ABRAHAM LINCOLN

★

People, Places, Politics: History in a Box

RESOURCE BOOK

General Editor: Steven Mintz, University of Houston
Senior Editors: Susan F. Saidenberg and Nicole Seary

Contributing Editors: David W. Blight, Gabor S. Boritt,
Richard Carwardine, Thavolia Glymph, Allen C. Guelzo,
Harold Holzer, Douglas L. Wilson

THE GILDER LEHRMAN
INSTITUTE *of* AMERICAN HISTORY
www.gilderlehrman.org

19 West 44th Street, Suite 500, New York, NY 10036

"People, Places, Politics: History in a Box" is made possible by a grant from
the Starr Foundation and a grant from the Julienne M. Michel Trust.

ISBN 978-1-932821-34-5

Foreword

The Gilder Lehrman Institute of American History is pleased to present *Abraham Lincoln: People, Places, Politics*, the second volume in our "History in a Box" series which began last year with *The Founding Era*. This initiative is the latest in an array of projects and publications the Institute offers, in fulfillment of its mission to serve students and teachers of American history across the country. The Institute now has programs in all 50 states, ranging from history high schools and teacher seminars, to partnerships in Teaching American History Grants. Our goal is eventually to be able to offer materials and support to every school and every history teacher in America.

Encouraged by the overwhelmingly positive response to *The Founding Era*, we set to work creating a multimedia resource focused on Abraham Lincoln. From his formative years, to his leadership during the Civil War, to his speeches and writings, to his transformative effect on American democracy, the essential elements of Lincoln's achievement are brought to life with primary sources and expert commentary from the very best scholars in the field. Teachers and students will experience some of the greatest Lincoln treasures in the renowned Gilder Lehrman Collection, including rare printings of the Emancipation Proclamation, original manuscripts of Lincoln speeches and letters, photographs by Matthew Brady, and other artifacts that inspire a sense of connection with the people and events of the time, and with the man himself.

Under the leadership of General Editor Steven Mintz, an all-star team of historians contributed commentary and editorial guidance to the contents of this box: David W. Blight (Class of 1954 Professor of American History Yale University), Gabor Boritt (Director of the Civil War Institute and Fluher Professor, Gettysburg College), Richard Carwardine (Rhodes Professor of American History, St. Catherines College, Oxford University), Thavolia Glymph (Assistant Professor of African and African American Studies and History, Duke University), Allen Guelzo (Henry R. Luce Professor of the Civil War Era and Professor of History, Gettysburg College), Harold Holzer (Co-chairman, United States Lincoln Bicentennial Commission), and Douglas L. Wilson (Co-director of the Lincoln Studies Center, Knox College).

Among the resources teachers will find here are:

- A resource book with short narrative summaries by the historians and extensive background materials, here published for the first time

- Classroom posters of Abraham Lincoln, Frederick Douglass, and the Emancipation Proclamation, among others

- Durable placards for classroom use, depicting historic figures and images

- A DVD with eight videotaped lectures by major historians such as David W. Blight, Richard Carwardine and James M. McPherson

- An interactive CD-ROM with soldiers' letters and Civil War songs and photographs

- A poster-sized timeline of all the major dates and events

These boxes will add to the resources of media centers and libraries, provide teachers with a rich variety of tools to enhance classroom presentations and lesson plans, and enable students to pursue research projects with greater access to primary materials. Uses will vary, but the overarching aim is to offer resources that will deepen every student's encounter with this profoundly important period of American history.

Over the many months since its germination, through its development and final production, the project has been shaped and led by Dr. Susan Saidenberg, Director of Exhibitions at the Gilder Lehrman Institute. The *Abraham Lincoln* resource box has benefited from the expert input of veteran history teachers Mike Serber, Steve Schwartz and Anthony Napoli, and from the research and editorial support of R. Benjamin Boerum, Nicole Seary, and Justine Ahlstrom. Our special thanks go to them, and to the Julienne M. Michel Trust for funds to support publication and distribution. As ever, we are grateful to the Co-Chairmen of the Institute, Richard Gilder and Lewis Lehrman, for their unflagging commitment to history education, especially to the classroom teachers who make it happen.

James G. Basker
President, Gilder Lehrman Institute of American History
Richard Gilder Professor of Literary History, Barnard College,
Columbia University

Lesley S. Herrmann
Executive Director, Gilder Lehrman Institute of American History

Acknowledgments

Special thanks to:

Scholars
Steven Mintz, David W. Blight, Gabor S. Boritt, Richard Carwardine, Thavolia Glymph, Allen C. Guelzo, Harold Holzer, Douglas L. Wilson, and James G. Basker

Institute staff
Susan F. Saidenberg, Lesley S. Herrmann, Sandra Trenholm, Justine Ahlstrom, Nicole Seary, and R. Benjamin Boerum

Production team
Production Coordinator: Masha Turchinsky
Design: Studio A

Organizations (for permission to reproduce materials)
Library of Congress, the Massachusetts Historical Society, the Morgan Library and Museum, the Huntington Library, McDougal Littell Inc., and the Division of Rare and Manuscript Collections at the Cornell University Library

Funders
The Altman Foundation, the Julienne M. Michel Trust, the Starr Foundation, the Lynde and Harry Bradley Foundation, the Cargill Foundation, the Fred and Mary Koch Foundation, the Eris & Larry Field Family Foundation, the Mary Alice Fortin Foundation, and the McInerney Family Foundation.

Founders of the Institute
Richard Gilder and Lewis Lehrman whose generosity and vision make possible all programs at the Gilder Lehrman Institute.

Contents

A Note to Educators

Abraham Lincoln: People, Places, Politics is the second volume in the *History in a Box* series — document-based resources that address critical themes and topics in American history. The Gilder Lehrman Institute developed the series in response to requests from educators for "teachable" materials. These resources reflect the Institute's mission to promote the study and love of American history.

Nothing can dispel apathy about the nation's past more powerfully than primary documents. Reading and interpreting the words of men and women who debated, fought, and in some cases died to save the Union will stir the imagination and engage students. Documents also encourage students to understand that the preservation of the nation, like more recent events, was neither inevitable nor uncontested: it was won at the cost of the deaths of 200,000 men and the assassination of the president. The boxes include primary sources from the Gilder Lehrman Collection, programmatic materials developed by the Institute, and documents from other repositories. Future boxes will include *Slavery and Abolition, Reconstruction,* and *The Progressive Era. Lincoln: People, Places, Politics* includes materials in varied media and formats, providing multiple points of entry to an investigation of the life and accomplishment of Lincoln as a politician and as president.

Scope and Themes

This volume of *History in Box* is organized around three themes: People, Places, and Politics. These themes infuse each of the eight chronological sections covered in the box. This thematic approach encourages students to examine the role of individuals, both famous and ordinary, in shaping the events of the Civil War era. For example, students investigating the emancipation of African Americans can compare a letter from soldier John Jones with the Emancipation Proclamation, as well as newspaper cartoons presenting opposing reactions to emancipation. Selective rather than comprehensive, the documents and ancillary components provide teachers with classroom-ready materials. We encourage teachers to log onto the Gilder Lehrman website: www.gilderlehrman.org, which has additional primary sources available for download, and to consult the other archives listed in the reference section of the Resource book component of this box.

Components

Abraham Lincoln offers the following components in a portable box:

- **A resource book** that provides historical background information on eight topics relating to Lincoln and the Civil War era, primary documents and artworks with annotations, maps, suggested multimedia resources for further study, and references. The documents, reproduced in facsimile and transcriptions, offer a flexible resource for teachers. Each document includes an annotation and can serve as a basis for classroom discussion. Teachers may also draw upon the grouping of documents and related material to develop an extended unit. Each chronological section includes a set of questions that refer to specific documents, to be used as a framework to enhance critical thinking and promote classroom discussions. (See the Table of Contents, pp vi-x. A CD-ROM with the contents of the book is included in the box.)

- *Mr. Lincoln's War, Selected Letters, Photographs, & Songs* with a guide to the contents. The interactive CD-ROM encourages students to assess the impact of the war and Lincoln's presidency on ordinary men and women.

- **A set of ten posters** that present a visual chronology of Lincoln and the Civil War, including portraits of Lincoln, handwritten drafts of his speeches, and photographs of Civil War soldiers and leaders.

- **Eight portrait placards** of key figures from the Civil War era with discussion questions for small-group work.

- **A poster-sized timeline** that allows students to place important milestones from the life of Lincoln within the context of national events.

- *Historians on the Record*, a DVD with eight lectures by leading scholars, including David W. Blight, Richard Carwardine and Allen C. Guelzo, discussing their books. Possible uses of these lectures include assigning groups of students to view three historians speaking about the same topic. Students can compare the respective interpretations and become acquainted with current historical scholarship.

While the resources in *Abraham Lincoln: People, Places, Politics* were primarily designed for use in high school classes, selected materials are suitable for use in grades four through eight. For example, students in middle school may enjoy and learn from the poster set as a visual record of Lincoln's era, as well as the songs, letters and photographs in *Mr. Lincoln's War*.

Goals for Student Learning

The Gilder Lehrman Institute is convinced that more students will be eager to learn history if they have a chance to work with original documents. *Abraham Lincoln: People, Places, Politics* provides teachers with a rich collection of primary sources, supplemented with annotations, guides, and multimedia resources. Our goals are that the *People, Places, Politics: History in a Box* series will:

Enhance students' ability to interpret and analyze primary source documents
The use of documents is transforming American history education. Increasingly, standardized history examinations test not only students' knowledge of the facts of American history but also their ability to read documents closely and analytically. The *History in a Box* series encourages students and teachers to examine the kinds of original documents that historians use to reconstruct the past.

Foster the ability to think critically and to synthesize multiple sources of information
Students will master historical facts, closely read and critically analyze primary-source documents, look at issues and problems from multiple perspectives, and articulate their findings in a coherent and logical manner. *History in a Box* is designed to help students develop skills in critical analysis they may apply to other disciplines or career challenges that they will face as adults.

Help students become informed citizens
Today historical study, like all education, is considered a lifelong process. Increasingly, adults must analyze, evaluate, and draw conclusions about modern events; they must ground their thinking in an informed understanding of the American past. The words of historian Arthur Schlesinger, Jr. summarize the critical relationship between informed citizens and a thriving democracy: "In the end a nation's history must be both the guide and the domain not so much of its historians as its citizens."

Susan F. Saidenberg, Project Director
Abraham Lincoln
People, Places, Politics: History in a Box

Introduction

More books have been written about Abraham Lincoln than any other figure in American history. There are more than 8,000 biographies and specialized books that explore various aspects of the sixteenth president's life. He continues to inspire and engage Americans two hundred years after his birth.

This collection of annotated primary sources uses letters, images, and documents to address the fascinating issues raised by Lincoln's life. How did a self-educated, rough-hewn lawyer with virtually no administrative experience become the savior of the Union? How did a proponent of colonization (the removal and relocation of former slaves) who told jokes that we would find racially offensive become a proponent, toward the end of his life, of suffrage for African American men? How did a young man known as a freethinker who rejected religious dogma come to write the Second Inaugural Address, with its powerful religious cadences and its Old Testament conception of a God who had brought war to punish America for the sin of slavery?

To truly appreciate Lincoln's significance, it is essential to look at the original sources, the letters, speeches, and other documents that he wrote. Only in this way can we begin to appreciate the difficult decisions that he made as president. His words have a simplicity, directness, and compression that approach poetry. Above all, by reading his writings we see how his views evolved over time. Much of Lincoln's greatness lay in his capacity for moral and political growth.

Individuals are shaped by, and often shape, the times in which they live. It seems inconceivable that the Confederacy might have won the Civil War, given the North's superiority in population, technology, and industry. Similarly, it strikes us as unimaginable that slavery might have persisted into the twentieth century. In fact, few, if any, historical developments are inevitable. In the end human actions make a huge difference. One cannot make sense of the outcome or meaning of the Civil War without reckoning with Abraham Lincoln.

SECTION I

★

Lincoln: The Formative Years

Lincoln: The Formative Years

by Douglas L. Wilson,
Co-director of the
Lincoln Studies Center,
Knox College

What American children learn about the early years of their greatest president, Abraham Lincoln, usually has to do with his "disadvantages" — that his family was poor, that he grew up in the backwoods without urban amenities, and that he had little formal schooling. While basically accurate, this traditional line of emphasis should give pause to teachers of history at the high school level. Not only is it already familiar to high school students, but, more importantly, the "disadvantages" approach has a primarily moral or admonitory purpose — it is ultimately more about teaching a lesson than about teaching history.

This is not to say, of course, that Lincoln's meager schooling cannot be a productive topic. The 1859 autobiographical sketch, for example, shows that Lincoln himself was keenly aware of his lack of schooling and appeared anxious to confess his educational liabilities. This description of his education, or lack thereof, offers rich opportunities for student investigation. What formal schooling did he actually have? How close was this to the norm? Any answer must take into account Lincoln's prodigious efforts at self-education, most of which were not school-related and can be traced as far back as his earliest boyhood. The evidence is overwhelming that Lincoln was a self-motivated learner who taught himself hard subjects such as grammar and mathematics long after his formal schooling ended. So why, it might be asked, did Lincoln, in his autobiographical statement, play up his lack of formal schooling and play down his self-education? This, in turn, leads to questions of context: what were the circumstances of his writing the autobiographical sketch, and what kind of impression was he trying to give? The effect of such an inquiry would thus be to relate the details of Lincoln's education and his formative years to his career as a successful politician.

Another liability of the "disadvantages" approach is that its presentation of facts is highly selective and draws a very narrow focus on Lincoln's early life. The perspective of history shows that Lincoln and his family, in these years, were direct participants in a number of significant historical events. They joined the westward movement, a nineteenth-century phenomenon that was driven by a variety of imperatives, from economic to religious. It was also a time that was characterized by a shift from small-scale agriculture to commercial enterprise, from primarily rural to town and urban life, from fixed occupations and opportunities to a more open and fluid society. Lincoln's formative years, as we see in the documents that follow, illustrate these and other unfolding historical developments. Encouraging students to see Abraham Lincoln in these contexts will help them to think historically.

Timeline

1809	_February 12_	Born in a one-room log cabin near Hodgenville, Kentucky, to Thomas Lincoln and Nancy Hanks Lincoln
1816	_December_	Lincoln's family moves to Spencer County, Indiana
1818	_October 5_	Lincoln's mother, Nancy Hanks Lincoln, dies
1819	_December 2_	Lincoln's father marries Sarah Bush Johnston, a widow with three children
1828	_April_	Takes a flatboat of farm produce to New Orleans where he is reported to have observed a slave auction
1830		Lincoln's family moves near Decatur, Illinois
		Gives his first political speech, calling for navigation improvements on the Sangamon River
1831	_April–July_	Makes a second flatboat trip to New Orleans
1831	_July_	Moves to New Salem, Illinois, where he works as a store clerk
1832		Elected captain of his rifle company during the Black Hawk War
		In his first election campaign, runs for Illinois General Assembly and loses
1833		Appointed postmaster of New Salem, and then deputy county surveyor

"Hon. Abraham Lincoln, Republican candidate, 1860," a print by Currier and Ives. (The Gilder Lehrman Collection, GLC 2132.01)

Springfield Dec. 20. 1859. J. W. Fell Esq, My dear Sir. Herewith is a little sketch, as you requested — There is not much of it, for the reason, I suppose, that there is not much of me — If anything be made out of it I wish it to be modest, and not to go beyond the material. If it were thought necessary to incorporate anything from any of my speeches, I suppose there would be no objection — Of course it must not appear to have been written by myself. Yours very truly, A. Lincoln.

Copied + catalogued

2166

Abraham Lincoln to Jesse W. Fell [copy in John Hay's hand], December 20, 1859. (Robert Todd Lincoln Collection, Library of Congress)

Lincoln's Cover Letter Sent with Autobiographical Sketch to the Chester County Times, *West Chester, Pa.*

December 20, 1859

In December 1859, Lincoln wrote an account of his life at the request of Jesse W. Fell, an Illinois Republican, for an article in the *Chester County Times*. The article later appeared with editorial additions on February 11, 1860.

Springfield, Dec. 20. 1859. J. W. Fell Esq, My dear Sir; Herewith is a little sketch, as you requested. There is not much of it, for the reason, I suppose, that there is not much of me. If anything be made out of it, I wish it to be modest, and not to go beyond the materials. If it were thought necessary to incorporate any thing from any of my speeches, I suppose there would be no objection. Of course it must not appear to have been written by myself. Yours very truly, A. Lincoln

I was born Feb. 12, 1809, in Hardin County, Kentucky. My parents were both born in Virginia, of undistinguished families — second families, perhaps I should say. My mother, who died in my tenth year, was of a family of the name of Hanks, some of whom now reside in Adams, and others in Macon Counties, Illinois. My paternal grandfather, Abraham Lincoln, emigrated from Rockingham County, Virginia, to Kentucky, about 1781 or 2, where, a year or two later, he was killed by indians, not in battle, but by stealth, when he was laboring to open a farm in the forest. His ancestors, who were quakers, went to Virginia from Berks County, Pennsylvania. An effort to identify them with the New-England family of the same name ended in nothing more definite, than a similarity of Christian names in both families, such as Enoch, Levi, Mordecai, Solomon, Abraham, and the like.

My father, at the death of his father, was but six years of age; and he grew up, litterally without education. He removed from Kentucky to what is now Spencer county, Indiana, in my eighth year. We reached our new home about the time the State came into the Union. It was a wild region, with many bears and other wild animals still in the woods. There I grew up. There were some schools, so called; but no qualification was ever required of a teacher, beyond "readin, writin, and cipherin" to the Rule of Three. If a straggler supposed to understand latin, happened to sojourn in the neighborhood, he was looked upon as a wizzard. There was absolutely nothing to excite ambition for education. Of course when I came of age I did not know much. Still somehow, I could read, write, and cipher to the Rule of Three; but that was all. I have not been to school since. The little advance I now have upon this store of education, I have picked up from time to time under the pressure of necessity.

I was raised to farm work, which I continued till I was twenty-two. At twenty one I came to Illinois, and passed the first year in Macon County. Then I got to New-Salem (at that time in Sangamon, now in Menard County, where I remained a year as a sort of Clerk in a store — then came the Black-Hawk war; and I was elected a Captain of Volunteers — a success which gave me more pleasure than any I have had since. I went the campaign, was elated, ran for the Legislature the same year (1832) and was beaten — the only time I ever have been beaten by the people. The next, and three succeeding biennial elections, I was elected to the Legislature. I was not a candidate afterwards. During this Legislative period I had studied law, and removed to Springfield to practice it. In 1846 I was once elected to the lower House of Congress. Was not a candidate for re-election. From 1849 to 1854, both inclusive, practiced law more assiduously than ever before. Always a whig in politics, and generally on the whig electoral tickets, making active canvasses — I was losing interest in politics, when the repeal of the Missouri Compromise aroused me again. What I have done since then is pretty well known.

If any personal description of me is thought desirable, it may be said, I am, in height, six feet, four inches, nearly; lean in flesh, weighing, on an average, one hundred and eighty pounds; dark complexion, with coarse black hair, and grey eyes — no other marks or brands recollected.

Lincoln the Lawyer

Before he became president, Abraham Lincoln supported himself and his family as an attorney. For twenty-four years, he was a lawyer who frequently traveled for up to six months a year, appearing for his clients at trials throughout Illinois's 8th Judicial Circuit, which spanned fourteen counties. He argued more than 300 criminal and civil appeals before the Illinois Supreme Court. Altogether, Lincoln probably handled over 5,000 legal cases.

Lincoln became one of Illinois's leading trial and appeals attorneys and he earned a substantial income from his legal practice, as much as $2,500 a year. He often represented the Illinois Central Railroad, but once when he billed the railroad $5,000 for successful work in an extraordinary case, the Illinois Central refused to pay. Lincoln had to go to court himself, where he won a judgment ordering the railroad to pay up.

He represented a wide range of clients. Some seventy-one times, he represented railroads, but in sixty-two cases, he represented clients who had been injured by railroads. His practice included cases involving contracts, debts, bankruptcies, and deeds. He and his partners even handled 110 divorces.

Lincoln's most famous criminal trial involved the 1858 prosecution of William "Duff" Armstrong for murder. An eyewitness claimed to have seen Armstrong fatally strike the victim after dark, but Lincoln used a farmer's almanac to demonstrate that the moonlight would have been too dim to allow the witness to see what he claimed on the night of the murder.

About thirty-four of Lincoln's cases dealt with slavery and race. In one, Lincoln defended a free woman of color accused of failing to repay a note, and in another, he helped secure the freedom of a fugitive slave. But Lincoln did not invariably take what we would consider the moral side in his cases. In 1847 he defended a slaveowner, whose slaves sued for their freedom on the grounds that they had been brought into Illinois, a free state, from Kentucky. In another case, he argued that a black woman and her child should be delivered to a client as repayment for a debt.

In notes prepared for a lecture in July 1850, Lincoln sums up his attitude toward the practice of law:

> There is a vague popular belief that lawyers are necessarily dishonest. I say <u>vague</u>, because when we consider to what extent <u>confidence</u> and <u>honors</u> are reposed in, and conferred upon lawyers by the people, it appears improbable that their <u>impression</u> of dishonesty, is very distinct and vivid. Yet the expression is common, almost universal. Let no young man choosing law for a calling, for a moment yield to this popular belief — resolve to be honest at all events; and if, in your own judgment, you can not be an honest

lawyer, resolve to be honest without being a lawyer. Choose some other occupation, rather than one in the choosing of which you do, in advance, consent to be a knave.

The letters on the following pages give vivid expression to the qualities that made Lincoln an effective attorney, including his wit, even temper, and facility with words.

Letter from Abraham Lincoln to James S. Irwin, Esq., November 2, 1842. (The Gilder Lehrman Collection, GLC 6256)

Abraham Lincoln to James S. Irwin Esq.

November 2, 1842

Jas. S. Irwin Esq:

Owing to my absence, yours of the 22nd. ult. was not received till this moment.

Judge Logan & myself are willing to attend to any business in the Supreme Court you may send us. As to fees, it is impossible to establish a rule that will apply in all, or even a great many cases. We believe we are never accused of being very unreasonable in this particular, and we would always be easily satisfied, provided we could see the money — but whatever fees we earn at a distance, if not paid <u>before</u>, we have noticed we never hear of after the work is done. We therefore are growing a little sensitive on that point.

Yours &tc.

A. Lincoln

Springfield, Ills. July 27. 1855

A.L. Brewer, Esq.

Dear Sir:

Yours of the 21st is received. When I wrote you in March, I explained to you the causes of the delay so far. When I went to that county in April, I did give the case my special attention. I commenced a suit in the Probate court, and as the executor would waive nothing, the time for trial extended beyond the term of the circuit court, and of course came on where I had to be elsewhere. However, my partner went up especially to attend to it, and when the trial (if it could be called a trial) was over, the Judge declined deciding then, but took the case under advisement. There was really nothing to decide, only the grave question whether the record, with the certificates, (which last, you remember we got up ourselves) proves the debt. And yet the Judge finally decided that against us!!! When the decision was made, we were notified by letter, and we sent up an appeal bond, to take the case to the circuit court, which sits again in September. Thus stands the case now.

Yours &c. A. Lincoln

Abraham Lincoln
to Anson L. Brewer

Springfield, Ills. July 27. 1855

July 27, 1855

A. L. Brewer, Esq.

Dear Sir:

Yours of the 21st is received. When I wrote you in March, I explained to you the causes of the delay so far. When I went to that county in April, I did give the case my special attention. I commenced a suit in the Probate court; and as the executor would waive nothing, the time for trial extended beyond the term of the circuit court, and of course [*struck:* have] came on when I had to be elsewhere. However, my partner went up especially to attend to it, and when the trial (if it could be called a trial) was over, the Judge declined deciding then, but took the case under advisement. There was really nothing to decide, only the <u>grave</u> question whether the record, with the certificates, (which last, you remember we got up ourselves) proves the debt. And yet the Judge finally decided that against us!!!. When the decision was made, we were notified by letter, and we sent up an appeal bond, to take the case to the circuit court, which sits again in September. Thus stands the case now.

Yours &c. A. Lincoln

Washington, Dec. 24th 1848-

My dear father:

Your letter of the 7th was received night before last. I very cheerfully send you the twenty dollars, which sum you say is necessary to save your land from sale. It is singular that you should have forgotten a judgment against you; and it is more singular that the plaintiff should have let you forget it so long, particularly as, I suppose you have always had property enough to satisfy a judgment of that amount. Before you pay it, it would be well to be sure you have not paid it; or at least, that you can not prove you have paid it. Give my love to Mother, and all the connections—

Affectionately your Son

A. Lincoln

Dear Johnston:

Your request for eighty dollars, I do not think it best to comply with now. At the various times when I have helped you a little, you have said to me "We can get along very well now" but in a very short time I find you in the same difficulty again. Now this can only happen by some defect in your conduct. What that defect is, I think I know. You are not lazy, and still you are an idler—

Lincoln's personal success in rising from humble origins shaped his outlook. He regarded the United States as a country where all people should have "an open field and a fair chance" to display their "industry enterprise and intelligence." This letter to his stepbrother stresses the habits of industry and self-improvement that characterized Lincoln himself.

Abraham Lincoln
to John D. Johnston

December 24, 1848

Dear Johnston:

    Your request for eighty dollars, I do not think it best, to comply with now. At the various times when I have helped you a little, you have said to me, "We can get along very well now," but in a very short time I find you in the same difficulty again. Now this can only happen by some defect in your <u>conduct</u>. What that defect is I think I know. You are not <u>lazy</u>, and still you <u>are</u> an <u>idler</u>. I doubt whether since I saw you, you have done a good whole day's work in any one day. You do not very much dislike to work; and still you do not work much, merely because it does not seem to you that you could get much for it. This habit of uselessly wasting time, is the whole difficulty; and it is vastly important to you, and still more so to your children, that you should break this habit. It is more important to them, because they have longer to live, and can keep out of an idle habit before they are in it; easier than they can get out after they are in.

You are now in need of some ready money; and what I propose is, that you shall go to work, "tooth and nails" for some body who will give you money [for] it. Let father and your boys take charge of things at home — prepare for a crop, and make the crop; and you go to work for the best money wages, or in discharge of any debt you owe, that you can get. And to secure you a fair reward for your labor, I now promise you, that for every dollar you will, between this and the first of next May, get for your own labor, either in money, or in your own indebtedness, I will then give you one other dollar. By this, if you hire yourself at ten dolla[rs] a month, from me you will get ten more, making twenty dollars a month for your work. In this, I do not mean you shall go off to St. Louis, or the lead mines, or the gold mines, in Calif[ornia], but I [mean for you to go at it for the best wages you] can get close to home [in] Coles county. Now if you will do this, you will soon be out of debt, and what is better, you will have a habit that will keep you from getting in debt again. But if I should now clear you out, next year you will be just as deep in as ever. You say you would almost give your place in Heaven for $70 or $80. Then you value your place in Heaven very cheaply for I am sure you can with the offer I make you get the seventy or eighty dollars for four or five months work. You say if I furnish you the money you will deed me the land, and, if you don't pay the money back, you will deliver possession. Nonsense! If you cant now live <u>with</u> the land, how will you then live without it? You have always been [kind] to me, and I do not now mean to be unkind to you. On the contrary, if you will but follow my advice, you will find it worth more than eight times eighty dollars to you.

Affectionately your brother,

A. Lincoln

During the 1860 presidential campaign, Lincoln's son Robert told his father that a friend had failed to pass the entrance exam required for admission to Harvard. Lincoln responded by writing a letter of encouragement to the young man, George C. Latham. This letter provides rare insight into the character of Abraham Lincoln, illustrating the determination that propelled him to rise from humble beginnings to the presidency of the United States. Latham ended up going to Yale.

Abraham Lincoln to George C. Latham

July 22, 1860

Springfield, Ills. July 22, 1860.

My dear George

I have scarcely felt greater pain in my life than on learning yesterday from Bob's letter, that you had failed to enter Harvard University. And yet there is very little in it, if you will allow no feeling of <u>discouragement</u> to seize, and prey upon you. It is a <u>certain</u> truth, that you <u>can</u> enter, and graduate in, Harvard University; and having made the attempt, you <u>must</u> succeed in it. "<u>Must</u>" is the word.

I know not how to aid you, save in the assurance of one of mature age, and much severe experience, that you <u>can</u> not fail, if you resolutely determine, that you <u>will</u> not.

The President of the institution, can scarcely be other than a kind man; and doubtless he would grant you an interview, and point out the readiest way to remove, or overcome, the obstacles which have thwarted you.

In your temporary failure there is no evidence that you may not yet be a better scholar, and a more successful man in the great struggle of life, than many others, who have entered college more easily.

Again I say let no feeling of discouragement prey upon you, and in the end you are sure to succeed.

With more than a common interest I subscribe myself

Very truly your friend.

A Lincoln.

Springfield, Ills. July 22. 1860.
My dear George,
              I have scarcely felt greater
pain in my life than on learning yesterday from Bob's letter, that you had
failed to enter Harvard University—
And yet there is very little in it,
if you will allow no feeling of
discouragement to seize, and prey
upon you— It is a certain truth, that
you can enter, and graduate in, Harvard University; and having made
the attempt, you must succeed in
it— "Must" is the word—
I know not how to aid you, save
in the assurance of one of mature
age, and much severe experience,
that you can not fail, if you resolutely determine, that you will not.
The President of the institution, can
scarcely be other than a kind man;

Letter from Abraham Lincoln to George C. Latham, July 22, 1860. Page 1.
(The Gilder Lehrman Collection, GLC 3876)

and doubtless he would grant you an interview, and point out the readiest way to remove, or overcome, the obstacles which have thwarted you—

In your temporary failure there is no evidence that you may not yet be a better scholar, and a more successful man in the great struggle of life, than many others, who have entered College more easily—

Again I say let no feeling of discouragement prey upon you, and in the end you are sure to succeed—

With more than a common interest I subscribe myself.

Very truly your friend.

A. Lincoln.

Letter from Abraham Lincoln to George C. Latham, July 22, 1860. Page 2.
(The Gilder Lehrman Collection, GLC 3876)

SECTION II

★

The Emergence of
Lincoln the Politician

The Emergence of Lincoln the Politician

by Richard Carwardine,
Rhodes Professor
of American History,
St. Catherine's College,
Oxford University

Lincoln's ambition, and hunger to make a mark in the world, gave him an appetite for politics. Those who knew Lincoln well could not miss his passionate yearning for public recognition. His law partner, William Herndon, judged that he was "the most ambitious man in the world." The idea of achieving self-fulfillment through politics struck him early on. His youthful reading included the *Life of George Washington* and William Scott's *Lessons in Elocution*. During his limited schooling in Indiana he wrote essays on politics and entertained his fellow pupils with public speaking. Politics, combined with the law, provided the best route to distinction in the developing western states. Elective office also provided a livelihood for a debt-ridden young man who possessed no formal qualifications, but had self-confidence, a good head for analysis, and a talent for public speaking.

Lincoln first ran for the Illinois legislature in 1832, aged only twenty-three. He was encouraged by New Salem community leaders impressed by his integrity, forceful mind, and folksy charm. "Every man is said to have his peculiar ambition," he told voters. "I have no other so great as that of being truly esteemed of my fellow men, by rendering myself worthy of their esteem." Defeated, he ran again in 1834, was elected, and stepped into a new world. He bought a suit and turned to the study of law. Over the next eight years he established himself as one of the state's foremost Whigs, and led the party in the House. Ambitious for national recognition, he sought his party's nomination for Congress and — despite disappointment in 1843 — became its candidate for the election of 1846, which he won with a handsome majority. Although his term in Washington proved undistinguished, he would have sought re-election in 1848 had it not been for the Whigs' principle of "rotation in office." Offered instead the governorship of Oregon Territory, Lincoln declined what he and his wife, Mary, considered a political dead-end. Rather, he returned to the law. Compared with his long-standing rival, Stephen A. Douglas, a star in the Democratic firmament, his career remained stubbornly grounded. But he did not stop yearning for public distinction. His chance came in 1854 with Douglas's Kansas-Nebraska Act, a thunderclap that transformed the nation's political weather.

The first two decades of Lincoln's public career coincided with the maturing of a mass democratic system, in which most white men had the vote. A key development was the emergence of recognizably modern political parties. Lincoln was a fine parliamentarian, as was evident in his masterly handling in the Illinois legislature of the bill to move the state capital to Springfield. But his special aptitude was for party building and the new electoral politics. With others, he set about organizing the Whig party into an effective electioneering force that — through committees and loyal newspapers — could identify and mobilize its supporters in every locality and precinct across the state.

Lincoln's approach to democratic politics was shaped by his experience of small western towns, face-to-face communities of generally no more than a few hundred inhabitants. He took the view that the people were sovereign and that American government rested on public opinion. The responsible politician could reshape and improve opinion by reasoned argument, and Lincoln had a well-judged confidence in his ability to connect with ordinary voters, through both the printed and the spoken word.

Lincoln's ambition was nourished by a vision of what the nation should be. His election addresses and his role in state and national legislatures offered what amounted to a consistent philosophy and political program. At its heart was a belief in the right of all individuals, through their industry, enterprise and self-discipline, to rise in an increasingly fluid and market-oriented society. Essential to his hopes for the poor were the nation's economic development and material advance. In Henry Clay's "American System" — comprising a national bank, a protective tariff, and better roads and waterways ("internal improvements") for transporting goods — Lincoln identified the essential means of the young Republic's economic development. Taken as a whole, the Whigs' program would speed the transition to a national market economy and draw ever more farmers and mechanics into the newly emerging commercial and industrial order.

The logic of Lincoln's economic thought was a social and moral order at odds with slavery. Lincoln opposed the Polk administration's war against Mexico, fearful that it would give slavery "new places to live in." But — no longer in political office — he accepted the compromise measures of 1850, which opened the possibility of slavery's expansion into parts of the Mexican cession, and which also included a more stringent Fugitive Slave Law. In 1854, however, Stephen Douglas's Kansas-Nebraska Act, by repealing the Missouri Compromise of 1820, opened up previously free territory on Illinois's western doorstep. Lincoln, roused to action in Springfield, delivered the greatest speech of his career to that date, setting out with stunning clarity the larger moral issues at stake in what he deemed Douglas's reversal of the "settled policy" of the Republic. Over the next six years, as he achieved national recognition, the essential elements of his argument did not change. They provided the rationale behind his contribution to building from the political debris of the mid-1850s a new Republican party: a political force dedicated to containing slavery within its existing limits and sustaining what Lincoln insisted was the Founders' vision of an ultimately slave-free republic.

Just as the elements that brought Lincoln to national attention — his remarkable blend of political skills and loyalty to a larger purpose — were not newly cast in the 1850s, so they would continue to mark his political course in the White House. Shrewd political management of the Union-Republican party coalition, allied to a tenacious defense of his vision for the nation, would be the hallmark of his presidency.

Timeline	**1834**	Begins to study law on his own
	August 4	The 25-year-old Lincoln is elected to the Illinois General Assembly as a member of the Whig party
	1836 *August 1*	Re-elected to the Illinois General Assembly (second term)
	September 9	Receives his law license
	1837 *April 15*	Moves from New Salem to Springfield, Illinois, and begins practicing law
	1838 *August 6*	Re-elected to the Illinois General Assembly (third term)
	1840 *August 3*	Re-elected to the Illinois General Assembly (fourth and final term)
	1842 *November 4*	Marries Mary Todd
	1843	Unsuccessfully seeks Whig nomination for U.S. House of Representatives
	August 1	His first child, Robert Todd Lincoln, is born
	1846 *March 10*	A son, Edward Baker Lincoln, is born
	August 3	Elected to the U.S. House of Representatives
	1847 *December 22*	Congressman Lincoln presents his "Spot Resolutions"
	1849 *May 22*	Receives U.S. Patent No. 6,469 for a device to raise boats over shoals
	1850 *February 1*	Son Edward dies
	December 21	His son William Wallace Lincoln (Willie) is born
	1853 *April 4*	His son Thomas (Tad) is born

1854		Elected to Illinois General Assembly but declines the seat to run for Senator
1855		Loses legislature's vote for U.S. Senate
1856	*February 22*	Takes lead organizing the Illinois Republican party
	June 19	Receives 110 votes for vice president at Republican National Convention
1857	*June 26*	Denounces U.S. Supreme Court Dred Scott decision
1858	*June 16*	Receives Republican nomination for U.S. Senate and delivers his "House Divided" speech
	August 21–October 15	Engages in seven debates with Stephen Douglas
1859	*January*	Illinois legislature selects Stephen Douglas for U.S. Senate over Lincoln

Lincoln the Whig Politician

Before he joined the Republican party, which emerged after the political explosion of the mid-1850s, Lincoln was a loyal Whig, who supported an active government role in promoting economic growth. He favored a protective tariff, a national bank, and federally funded internal improvements. Like other Whigs, Lincoln was a strong advocate of technological innovation. Indeed, he was the only president to receive a patent, for an 1849 device to lift boats over shoals.

Like many other Whigs, he owed his political allegiance not to his state, region, or ethnic background, but to being an American. And he defined Americanism in terms of a commitment to the ideas of freedom, equality, and unity. Like Daniel Webster, another Whig politician, Lincoln regarded liberty and union as one and inseparable. But as he explained in a speech in New York in 1861, the Union was valuable because it promoted "the prosperity and liberty of the people."

Elected as a Whig to Congress in 1846, Lincoln gained local notoriety when he lashed out against the Mexican War, calling it immoral, proslavery, and a threat to the nation's republican values. President James K. Polk had called for war, accusing Mexico of shedding "American blood on American soil." Lincoln responded by introducing a series of resolutions demanding to know the "particular spot of soil on which the blood of our citizens was so shed." One of Lincoln's constituents branded him "the Benedict Arnold of our district," and he lost favor with his own party. The Whigs' "reciprocity agreement," which Lincoln had earlier championed, prevented him from standing again for Congress.

Abraham Lincoln,
"Spot Resolutions"

December 22, 1847

Whereas the President of the United States, in his message of May 11, 1846, has declared that "the Mexican Government not only refused to receive him [the envoy of the United States], or listen to his propositions, but, after a long-continued series of menaces, has at last invaded our territory and shed the blood of our fellow-citizens on our own soil:"

And again, in his message of December 8, 1846, that "we had ample cause of war against Mexico long before the breaking out of hostilities; but even then we forbore to take redress into our own hands until Mexico herself became the aggressor, by invading our soil in hostile array, and shedding the blood of our citizens:"

And yet again, in his message of December 7, 1847, that "the Mexican Government refused even to hear the terms of adjustment which he [our minister of peace] was authorized to propose, and finally, under wholly unjustifiable pretexts, involved the two countries in war, by invading the territory of the State of Texas, striking the first blow, and shedding the blood of our citizens on our own soil."

And whereas this House is desirous to obtain a full knowledge of all the facts which go to establish whether the particular spot on which the blood of our citizens was so shed was or was not at that time our own soil: Therefore, Resolved By the House of Representatives, That the President of the United States be respectfully requested to inform this House —

1st. Whether the spot on which the blood of our citizens was shed, as in his messages declared, was or was not within the territory of Spain, at least after the treaty of 1819, until the Mexican revolution.

2d. Whether that spot is or is not within the territory which was wrested from Spain by the revolutionary Government of Mexico.

3d. Whether that spot is or is not within a settlement of people, which settlement has existed ever since long before the Texas revolution, and until its inhabitants fled before the approach of the United States army.

4th. Whether that settlement is or is not isolated from any and all other settlements by the Gulf and the Rio Grande on the south and west, and by wide uninhabited regions on the north and east.

5th. Whether the people of that settlement, or a majority of them, or any of them, have ever submitted themselves to the government or laws of Texas or the United States, by consent or compulsion, either by accepting office, or voting at elections, or paying tax, or serving on juries, or having process served upon them, or in any other way.

6th. Whether the people of that settlement did or did not flee from the approach of the United States army, leaving unprotected their homes and their growing crops, before the blood was shed, as in the messages stated; and whether the first blood, so shed, was or was not shed within the enclosure of one of the people who had thus fled from it.

7th. Whether our citizens, whose blood was shed, as in his message declared, were or were not, at that time, armed officers and soldiers, sent into that settlement by the military order of the President, through the Secretary of War.

8th. Whether the military force of the United States was or was not sent into that settlement after General Taylor had more than once intimated to the War Department that, in his opinion, no such movement was necessary to the defence or protection of Texas.

Photograph of the U.S. Capitol, Washington, D.C., 1846. (Library of Congress Prints and Photographs Division)

Lincoln and Sectional Conflict

During the late 1840s, massive immigration from Ireland and Germany led to an outburst of anti-immigrant and anti-Catholic sentiment in the United States. Between 1846 and 1855, more than three million immigrants arrived in America. Nativists — ardent opponents of immigration — formed the American Party, vigorously opposed to immigrants and Catholics. The party received its nickname, the "Know-Nothings," from the fact that when members were asked about the workings of the party, they were supposed to reply, "I know nothing."

In the presidential election of 1856, the party supported Millard Fillmore and won more than twenty-one percent of the popular vote and eight electoral votes. In Congress, the party boasted five senators and forty-three representatives. Between 1853 and 1855, the Know-Nothings replaced the Whigs as the nation's second largest party.

The passage of the Kansas-Nebraska Act in 1854 precipitated bloody confrontations in Kansas as pro-slavery settlers from Missouri fought free-soil settlers and abolitionists. After the passage of the Act, Lincoln reentered politics. In the North the Know-Nothing party was supplanted by a new and explosive sectional party, the Republicans. By 1856 northern workers felt more threatened by the southern slave power than by Catholic immigrants. At the same time, fewer and fewer southerners were willing to support a party that ignored the question of the expansion of slavery. As a result, the Know-Nothing party rapidly dissolved.

Abraham Lincoln was an ardent opponent of nativism. He regarded immigrants as a "replenishing stream," the "flesh of the flesh of the men who wrote" the Declaration of Independence. In this letter, written in 1855, he privately denounced the Know-Nothings in eloquent terms.

*Excerpt from
a Letter from
Abraham Lincoln
to Joshua Speed*

August 24, 1855

Letter from Abraham Lincoln to Joshua Speed, August 24, 1855. (Massachusetts Historical Society, MHS 1634)

. . . I am not a Know-Nothing. That is certain. How could I be? How can any one who abhors the oppression of negroes, be in favor of degrading classes of white people? Our progress in degeneracy appears to me to be pretty rapid. As a nation, we began by declaring that "<u>all</u> <u>men</u> <u>are</u> <u>created</u> <u>equal</u>." We now practically read it "all men are created equal, <u>except</u> <u>negroes</u>." When the Know-Nothings get control, it will read "all men are created equal, except negroes, <u>and</u> <u>foreigners,</u> <u>and</u> <u>Catholics</u>". When it comes to this I should prefer emigrating to some country where they make no pretence of loving liberty — to Russia, for instance, where despotism can be taken pure, and without the base alloy of hypocracy.

Mary will probably pass a day or two in Louisville in October. My kindest regards to Mrs. Speed. On the leading subject of this letter, I have more of her sympathy than I have of yours. And yet let [me] say I am

Your friend forever   A. Lincoln

Lincoln the Republican Politician

After joining the Republican party, Lincoln encouraged party members to focus their attention on a single unifying issue — opposition to the expansion of slavery into the western territories — rather than divide their strength by advocating too many issues. Persistence in pursuit of this goal helped make Lincoln an acceptable Republican presidential candidate in 1860.

The Republican party was a coalition of very diverse groups. It included former Whigs who wanted to see slavery confined to the states where it was legal; northern Democrats who were tired of a party where southern slaveholders called all the shots; outright abolitionists who wanted to see slavery outlawed; and even a scattering of Know-Nothings. Despite their differences, all of these groups shared a conviction that the western territories should be saved for free labor. "Free labor, free soil, free men," was the Republican slogan. Lincoln himself was a staunch defender of free labor, a "just and generous, and prosperous system, which opens the way for all, gives hope to all, and energy, and progress, and improvement of condition to all."

This speech fragment shows Lincoln's extraordinary power as a writer and speaker. He articulates two principles that informed his vision: that slavery, no matter how legal it was on Southern statute books, was a violation of natural law, and that made it wrong in moral terms; and that the real purpose of law ought to be to help people to self-improvement by creating equality of opportunity for all. Looking back to the Declaration of Independence, Lincoln based his opposition to slavery on the principles of American democracy. Lincoln's vision was of an America where all are entitled to the fruits of their labor.

dent truth— Made so plain by our good Father in Heaven, that all feel and understand it, even down to brutes and creeping insects— The ant, who has toiled and dragged a crumb to his nest, will furiously defend the fruit of his labor, against whatever robber snails him— So plain, that the most dumb and stupid slave that ever toiled for a master, does constantly know that he is wronged— So plain that no one, high or low, ever does mistake it, except in a plainly selfish way; for although volume upon volume is written to prove slavery a very good thing, we never hear of the man who wishes to take the good of it, by being a slave himself—

Most governments have been based, practically, on the denial of the equal rights of men, as I have, in part, stated them; ours began, by affirming those rights— They said, some men are too ignorant, and vicious, to share in government— Possibly so, said we; and, by your system, you would always keep them ignorant, and vicious— We proposed to give all a chance; and we expected the weak to grow stronger, the ignorant, wiser; and all better, and happier together—

We made the experiment; and the fruit is before us— Look at it— think of it— Look at it, in its aggregate grandeur, of extent of country, and number of population— of ships, and steamboat, and rail—

Note by Abraham Lincoln for a speech on slavery and American government, c. 1857-1858.
(The Gilder Lehrman Collection, GLC 3251)

Abraham Lincoln on Slavery and American Government

c. 1857-1858

. . . Made so plain by our good Father in Heaven, that all <u>feel</u> and <u>understand</u> it, even down to brutes and creeping insects. The ant, who has toiled and dragged a crumb to his nest, will furiously defend the fruit of his labor, against whatever robber assails him. So plain, that the most dumb and stupid slave that ever toiled for a master, does constantly <u>know</u> that he is wronged. So plain that no one, high or low, ever does mistake it, except in a plainly <u>selfish</u> way; for although volume upon volume is written to prove slavery a very good thing, we never hear of the man who wishes to take the good of it, <u>by</u> <u>being a</u> <u>slave</u> <u>himself</u>.

<u>Most</u> <u>governments</u> have been based, practically, on the denial of the equal rights of men, as I have, in part, stated them; <u>ours</u> began, by <u>affirming</u> those rights. <u>They</u> said, some men are too <u>ignorant</u>, and <u>vicious</u>, to share in government. Possibly so, said we; and, by your system, you would always keep them ignorant, and vicious. We proposed to give <u>all</u> a chance; and we expected the weak to grow stronger, the ignorant, wiser; and all better, and happier together.

We made the experiment; and the fruit is before us. Look at it — think of it. Look at it, in its aggregate grandeur, of extent of country, and numbers of population — of ship, and steamboat, and rail-[road.]

*The "House
Divided" Speech*

By 1850, the extension of slavery into the new territories won through the
Mexican War of 1846–48 provided a testing ground for competing visions of
America. The passage of the Fugitive Slave Law in 1850 and the Kansas-
Nebraska Act in 1854 precipitated a firestorm in Kansas.

The Dred Scott decision in 1857 affirmed that no slave or descendant of a
slave could ever be a U.S. citizen. It ignited jubilation in the South and fierce
protests in the North, and marked the end of compromise between the opposing groups. The decision strengthened the bonds among abolitionists,
Republicans, and moderates in the North.

All these events moved Lincoln to take a public stand against the extension
of slavery. In this speech fragment from 1857, which he later expanded as the
opening speech of the 1858 campaign against Stephen Douglas, Abraham Lincoln identifies slavery as a moral and a political issue that threatened the
continued existence of the United States. Invoking the famous biblical words,
"A house divided against itself can not stand," he declared "I believe this government can not endure permanently half slave, and half free." Lincoln's
formulation was viewed by some as radical and provocative. However, in this
speech Lincoln appeals to a growing sense in the North that national politics
under successive Democratic administrations (aided by a southwards leaning
Supreme Court) were being driven by a slave interest, which many northerners
were increasingly ready to call the Slave Power.

Why, Kansas is neither the whole, nor a
tithe of the real question—

"A house divided against itself can not
stand."

I believe this government can not endure
permanently, half slave, and half free—

I expressed this belief a year ago; and
subsequent developments, have but confirmed me.

I do not expect the Union to be dissolved—I do not expect the house to fall; but
I do expect it will cease to be divided—It
will become all one thing, or all the other—Either
the opponents of slavery will arrest the further spread
of it, and put it in course of ultimate extinction; or
its advocates will push it forward till, it shall become alike lawful in all the states, old, as well
as new—Do you doubt it? Study the Dred Scott
decision, and then see, how little, even now, remains
to be done—

That decision may be reduced to three points—
The first is, that a negro can not be a citizen—
That point is made in order to deprive the negro
in every possible event, of the benefit of that provision of the U. S Constitution which declares that;
"The citizens of each State shall be entitled to
all privileges and immunities of citizens in the
several States"

The second point is, that the U. S constitution protects slavery, as property, in all the U. S. territories, and
that neither congress, nor the people of the territories,
nor any other power, can prohibit it, at any time pri-
or to the formation of State constitutions—

This point is made, in order that the territories may
safely be filled up with slaves, before the formation of
State constitutions, and thereby to embarrass the free state

Notes by Abraham Lincoln for the "House Divided" speech, December 1857.
(The Gilder Lehrman Collection, GLC 2533)

Why, Kansas is neither the <u>whole</u>, nor a <u>tithe</u> of the real question.

"A house divided against itself can not stand"

I believe this government can not endure permanently, half slave, and half free.

I expressed this belief a year ago; and subsequent developments have but confirmed me.

I do not expect the Union to be dissolved. I do not expect the house to fall; but I <u>do</u> expect it will cease to be divided. It will become <u>all</u> one thing, or <u>all</u> the other. Either the opponents of slavery will arrest the further spread of it, and put it in course of ultimate extinction; or its advocates will push it forward till it shall become alike lawfull in <u>all</u> the states, old, as well as new. Do you doubt it? Study the Dred Scott decision, and then see, how little, even now, remains to be done.

That decision may be reduced to three points. The first is, that a negro can not be a citizen. That point is made in order to deprive the negro in every possible event, of the benefit of that provision of the U. S Constitution which declares that: "The <u>citizens</u> of each State shall be entitled to all previleges and immunities of citizens in the several States."

The second point is, that the U. S constitution protects slavery, as property, in all the U. S. territories, and that neither congress, nor the people of the territories, nor any other power, can prohibit it, at any time prior to the formation of State constitutions.

This point is made, in order that the territories may safely be filled up with slaves, <u>before</u> the formation of State constitutions, and thereby to embarrass the free states[.]

The Lincoln-Douglas Debates

The critical issues dividing the nation — slavery versus free labor, popular sovereignty, and the legal and political status of black Americans — were brought into sharp focus in the 1858 Illinois Senate campaign. Senator Stephen A. Douglas, the frontrunner for the Democratic presidential nomination in 1860, and Abraham Lincoln, the emerging voice of the Republican party in the west, fiercely debated.

Lincoln and Douglas crisscrossed Illinois, traveling nearly 10,000 miles in seven face-to-face debates before crowds of up to 15,000. Douglas pictured Lincoln as a fanatical "Black Republican" and "amalgamationist" whose goal was to incite civil war, emancipate the slaves, and make blacks the social and political equals of whites. Lincoln denied that he was a radical. He supported the Fugitive Slave Law and opposed any interference with slavery in the states where it already existed. Lincoln was not in favor "of bringing about in any way the social and political equality of the white and black races." But he also argued that slavery was morally repugnant and was emphatically opposed to its extension.

During the course of the debates, Lincoln and Douglas presented two contrasting views of the problem of slavery. Douglas argued that slavery was a dying institution that had reached its natural limits. The problem of slavery could best be resolved if it were treated as essentially a local problem. Lincoln regarded slavery as a dynamic, expansionistic institution, hungry for new territory. If northerners allowed slavery to spread unchecked, slave owners would make slavery a national institution.

The candidates clashed dramatically over the issue of black Americans' rights. Douglas was unalterably opposed to black civil and natural rights. "I want citizenship for whites only," he declared. Lincoln also opposed full civil rights for free blacks but insisted that black Americans were the natural equals of Douglas and "every living man" in their right to life, liberty, and the fruits of their own labor. Although Lincoln lost in the legislature to Douglas, the debates gave him a national presence. Lincoln himself noted his defeat was "a slip and not a fall."

The following speech fragment is one of the few surviving Lincoln manuscripts from the period of the Lincoln-Douglas debates. Speaking to voters, Lincoln recalled the long struggle to abolish slavery in Great Britain. He observed that the abolition of slavery "may not be completely attained within . . . the term of my [natural] life. . . . Even in this view, I am proud, in my passing speck of time, to contribute an humble mite to that glorious consummation, which my own poor eyes may not last to see."

I have never professed an indifference to the honors of official station; and were I to do so now, I should only make myself ridiculous. Yet I have never failed— do not now fail— to remember that in the republican cause there is a higher aim than that of mere office— I have not allowed myself to forget that the abolition of the Slave-trade by Great Brittain, was agitated a hundred years before it was a final success; that the measure had its open fire-eating opponents; its stealthy "dont care" opponents; its dollar and cent opponents; its inferior race opponents; its negro equality opponents; and its religion and good order opponents; that all these opponents got offices, and their adversaries got none— But I have also remembered that, though they blazed, like tallow-candles for a century, at last they flickered in the socket, died out, stank in the dark for a brief season, and were remembered no more, even by the smell— School-boys know that Wilbeforce, and Granville Sharpe, helped that cause forward; but who can now name a single man who labored to retard it? Remembering these things I can not but regard it as possible that the higher object of this contest may not be completely attained within

Notes by Abraham Lincoln for a speech concerning the abolition of slavery, c. July 1858.
(The Gilder Lehrman Collection, GLC 5302)

the term of my natural life. But I can not doubt either that it will come in due time. Even in this view, I am proud, in my passing speck of time, to contribute an humble mite to that glorious consummation, which my own poor eyes may not last to see —

I have never professed an indifference to the honors of official station; and were I to do so now, I should only make myself ridiculous. Yet I have never failed — do not now fail — to remember that in the republican cause there is a higher aim than that of mere office. I have not allowed myself to forget that the abolition of the Slave-trade by Great Brittain, was agitated a hundred years before it was a final success; that the measure had it's open fire-eating opponents; it's stealthy "don't care" opponents; it's dollar and cent opponents; it's inferior race opponents; its negro equality opponents; and its religion and good order opponents; that all these opponents got offices, and their adversaries got none. But I have also remembered that [inserted: though] they blazed, like tallow-candles for a century, at last they flickered in the socket, died out, stank in the dark for a brief season, and were remembered no more, even by the smell. School-boys know that Wilbe[r]force, and Granville Sharpe, helped that cause forward; but who can now name a single man who labored to retard it? Remembering these things I can not but regard it as possible that the higher object of this contest may not be completely attained within the term of my [inserted: natural] life. But I can not doubt either that it will come in due time. Even in this view, I am proud, in my passing speck of time, to contribute an humble mite to that glorious consummation, which my own poor eyes may [struck: never] [inserted: not] last to see.

SECTION III

★

Lincoln and the Election of 1860

Lincoln and the Election of 1860

by Harold Holzer, Co-chairman of the United States Lincoln Bicentennial Commission

In 1858, a few weeks after he lost the U.S. Senate race to Stephen A. Douglas, Abraham Lincoln wrote to assure one of his supporters: "Another explosion will come before a great while." Two years later, the explosion came: one of the most bitterly contested, divisive, and raucous presidential elections in American history.

Senator Douglas was widely expected to win the Democratic nomination. But during the 1858 debates, he had expressed the view that just new territories should be allowed to vote to permit slavery. Existing states — including ones in the South — could vote to ban slavery. No one believed this would happen, but the sentiment helped doom Douglas's chances of securing his party's presidential nod. Democrats ultimately split, unable to decide on a single nominee: the Northern faction chose Douglas, and the Southern one nominated John C. Breckinridge, the incumbent vice president. A splinter Constitutional Union party nominated former Senator John Bell of Tennessee. The Republicans were widely expected to choose Senator William H. Seward of New York. But over-confident Seward forces underestimated the momentum for nominating a westerner. On the third ballot, Lincoln won the Republican nomination in a major upset.

Presidential candidates did not customarily campaign on their own behalf in the mid-nineteenth century and Douglas was criticized for breaking tradition in doing so. Lincoln, on the other hand, remained at home, content to let supporters march in exuberant torchlight parades, distribute flattering pictures, broadsides, and campaign pins, and reprint and circulate his speeches. The Republican campaign cleverly emphasized Lincoln's humble origins — including his already legendary prowess as a rail-splitter — and kept as quiet as possible about divisive issues like slavery. During the entire five-and-a-half-month campaign, Lincoln spoke but once: briefly, and merely to express his thanks, to a rally at his Springfield home in August.

The November 8 election results reflected the sharp regional divisions plaguing the nation. Lincoln won every Northern state but New Jersey, gaining a majority 180 electoral votes though he attracted less than forty percent of the popular votes. Breckinridge won seventy-two electoral votes, all in the South, in most of which Lincoln's name did not even appear on the ballots. Bell won thirty-nine votes, and Douglas, though he came in second in the popular vote, only twelve. More than eighty percent of the eligible voters — all white males, of course — participated in the hotly contested election, one of the highest turnouts ever.

Timeline

1860   *February 27*   Cooper Institute (Union) address in New York

May 18   Wins Republican party nomination for president

November 6   Elected president with 180 of 303 electoral votes and nearly forty percent of the popular vote

December 20   South Carolina secedes from the Union

The Cooper Institute Address

Before the Republican National Convention, Lincoln delivered a speech on February 27, 1860, at the Cooper Institute — now Cooper Union — in New York City. Despite his rustic manners, awkward gait, and ill-fitting trousers and coat, he won over the crowd that evening with the power of his intellect and his engaging, closely argued prose. It was this speech that thrust him onto the national stage and transformed him into a contender for the 1860 Republican presidential nomination. On May 18, 1860, Lincoln was nominated for president at the Republican National Convention in Chicago.

In the segment below Lincoln asserts, responding to a previous speech by Douglas, that Congress has the authority to restrict the spread of slavery into the federal territories. Drawing upon detailed research, he shows that twenty-one of the thirty-nine signers of the U.S. Constitution believed that Congress had the power to restrict slavery. He also makes it clear that John Brown's raid on Harper's Ferry was not a Republican plot and maintains that Republicans had no desire to interfere with slavery as it existed in the Southern states.

THE

ADDRESS

OF THE

HON. ABRAHAM LINCOLN,

IN INDICATION OF

THE POLICY OF THE FRAMERS OF THE CONSTITUTION AND THE PRINCIPLES
OF THE REPUBLICAN PARTY,

Delivered at Cooper Institute, February 27th, 1860,

ISSUED BY

THE YOUNG MEN'S REPUBLICAN UNION,

(659 BROADWAY, NEW-YORK,)

WITH NOTES BY

CHARLES C. NOTT & CEPHAS BRAINERD,

Members of the Board of Control.

NEW-YORK:
GEORGE F. NESBITT & CO., PRINTERS AND STATIONERS.
1860.

Title page of an 1860 pamphlet reprinting Abraham Lincoln's Cooper Institute Address, New York, NY, February 27, 1860. (The Gilder Lehrman Collection, GLC 533)

Mr. President and fellow citizens of New York:

What is the frame of government under which we live?

The answer must be: "The Constitution of the United States." That Constitution consists of the original, framed in 1787, (and under which the present government first went into operation,) and twelve subsequently framed amendments, the first ten of which were framed in 1789.

Who were our fathers that framed the Constitution? I suppose the "thirty-nine" who signed the original instrument may be fairly called our fathers who framed that part of the present Government. It is almost exactly true to say they framed it, and it is altogether true to say they fairly represented the opinion and sentiment of the whole nation at that time. Their names, being familiar to nearly all, and accessible to quite all, need not now be repeated.

I take these "thirty-nine," for the present, as being "our fathers who framed the Government under which we live."

What is the question which, according to the text, those fathers understood "just as well, and even better than we do now?"

It is this: Does the proper division of local from federal authority, or anything in the Constitution, forbid our Federal Government to control as to slavery in our Federal Territories? . . .

After presenting evidence that 21 of the 39 signers of the Constitution held that Congress had the power to restrict slavery in the federal territories, Lincoln proceded to rebut the charge that the Republican party endorsed John Brown's raid on the federal arsenal at Harper's Ferry, Virginia.

You charge that we stir up insurrections among your slaves. We deny it; and what is your proof? Harper's Ferry! John Brown!! John Brown was no Republican; and you have failed to implicate a single Republican in his Harper's Ferry enterprise. If any member of our party is guilty in that matter, you know it or you do not know it. If you do know it, you are inexcusable for not designating the man and proving the fact. If you do not know it, you are inexcusable for asserting it, and especially for persisting in the assertion after you have tried and failed to make the proof. You need to be told that persisting in a charge which one does not know to be true, is simply malicious slander. . . .

Republican doctrines and declarations are accompanied with a continual protest against any interference whatever with your slaves, or with you about your slaves. Surely, this does not encourage them to revolt. True, we do, in common with "our fathers, who framed the Government under which we live," declare our belief that slavery is wrong; but the slaves do not hear us declare even this. For anything we say or do, the slaves would scarcely know there is a Republican party. I believe they would not, in fact, generally know it but for your misrepresentations of us, in their hearing. In your political contests among yourselves, each faction charges the other with sympathy with Black Republicanism; and then, to give point to the charge, defines Black Republicanism to simply be insurrection, blood and thunder among the slaves. . . .

John Brown's effort was peculiar. It was not a slave insurrection. It was an attempt by white men to get up a revolt among slaves, in which the slaves refused to participate. In fact, it was so absurd that the slaves, with all their ignorance, saw plainly enough it could not succeed. That affair, in its philosophy, corresponds with the many attempts, related in history, at the assassination of kings and emperors. An enthusiast broods over the oppression of a people till he fancies himself commissioned by Heaven to liberate them. He ventures the attempt, which ends in little else than his own execution. Orsini's attempt on Louis Napoleon, and John Brown's attempt at Harper's Ferry were, in their philosophy, precisely the same. The eagerness to cast blame on old England in the one case, and on New England in the other, does not disprove the sameness of the two things. . . .

Wrong as we think slavery is, we can yet afford to let it alone where it is, because that much is due to the necessity arising from its actual presence in the nation; but can we, while our votes will prevent it, allow it to spread into the National Territories, and to overrun us here in these Free States? If our sense of duty forbids this, then let us stand by our duty, fearlessly and effectively. Let us be diverted by none of those sophistical contrivances wherewith we are so industriously plied and belabored — contrivances such as groping for some middle ground between the right and the wrong, vain as the search for a man who should be neither a living man nor a dead man — such as a policy of "don't care" on a question about which all true men do care — such as Union appeals beseeching true Union men to yield to Disunionists, reversing the divine rule, and calling, not the sinners, but the righteous to repentance — such as invocations to Washington, imploring men to unsay what Washington said, and undo what Washington did.

Neither let us be slandered from our duty by false accusations against us, nor frightened from it by menaces of destruction to the Government nor of dungeons to ourselves. LET US HAVE FAITH THAT RIGHT MAKES MIGHT, AND IN THAT FAITH, LET US, TO THE END, DARE TO DO OUR DUTY AS WE UNDERSTAND IT.

The following two images are details from a broadside depicting the United States as the Civil War broke out, crystallizing the division between free and slave states. Lincoln is shown with Gen. Winfield and Major Robert Anderson, commander at Fort Sumter. Thirty-one million people lived in the United States, of whom 4,700,000 white males voted in the 1860 election. Lincoln received not a single recorded vote in Alabama, Arkansas, Georgia, South Carolina, North Carolina, Florida, Texas, Mississippi, Tennessee, and Virginia.

Popular Vote for President, 1860.

	Rep. Lincoln.	Dem. Douglas.	Dem. Breck'ge.	Union. Bell.
Alabama.....	....	13,651	48,831	27,875
Arkansas....	....	5,227	28,732	20,094
California....	39,173	38,516	34,334	6,817
Connecticut..	43,792	15,522	14,641	*3,291
Delaware....	3,815	1,023	7,337	3,864
Florida......	....	367	8,543	5,437
Georgia......	....	11,590	51,889	42,886
Illinois	172,161	160,215	2,404	4,913
Indiana......	139,033	115,509	12,295	5,306
Iowa........	70,409	55,111	1,048	1,763
Kentucky....	1,364	25,651	53,143	66,058
Louisiana....	....	7,625	22,681	20,204
Maine.......	62,811	26,693	6,368	2,046
Maryland....	2,294	5,966	42,482	41,760
Massachusetts	106,533	34,372	5,939	22,331
Michigan.....	88,480	65,057	805	405
Minnesota....	22,069	11,920	748	62
Mississippi...	....	3,283	40,797	25,040
Missouri.	17,028	58,801	31,317	58,372
N. Hampshire	37,519	25,881	2,112	441
New Jersey..	58,324	*62,801	....	....
New York....	353,804	*303,329	....	....
North Carolina	....	2,701	48,539	44,990
Ohio........	231,610	187,232	11,405	12,194
Oregon......	5,270	3,951	5,006	183
Pennsylvania.	268,030	16,765	*178,871	12,776
Rhode Island.	12,244	*7,707	....	....
South Carolina	Electors	chosen	by Legi	slature.
Tennessee....	....	11,350	64,709	69,274
Texas........	....	....	47,548	*15,438
Vermont.....	33,808	6,849	218	1,969
Virginia	1,929	16,200	74,323	74,681
Wisconsin....	86,110	65,021	888	161
Total.......	1,857,610	1,365,976	847,953	590,631

* Fusion.

"Popular Vote for President, 1860," detail from *Lloyd's New Political Chart.* (The Gilder Lehrman Collection, GLC 4243)

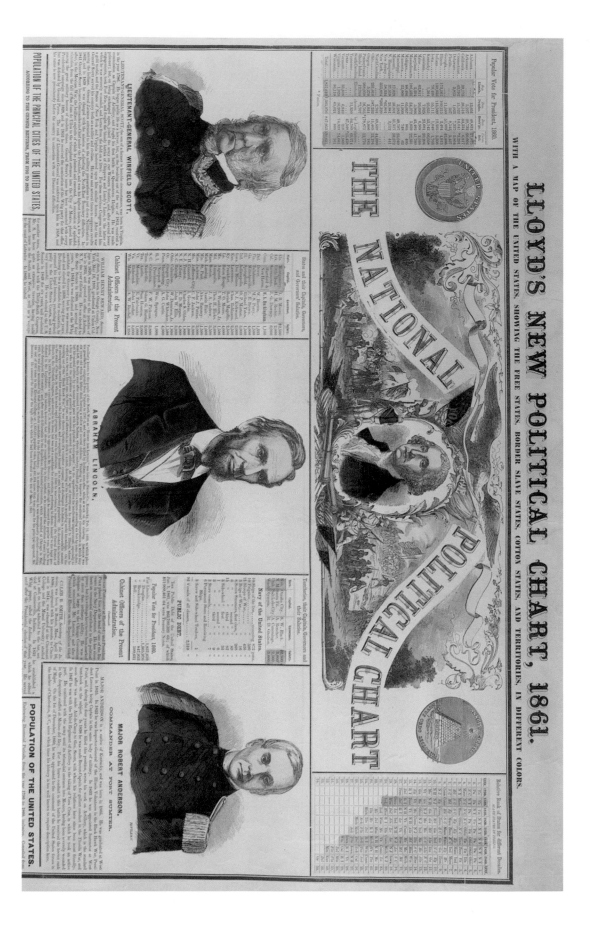

Biographies of Lincoln and two military leaders, plus national statistics from *Lloyd's New Political Chart, 1861* (The Gilder Lehrman Collection, GLC 4243)

Leaving Springfield

Rain was falling on the morning of February 11, 1861, when Lincoln stood on the rear car of a train and bid farewell to his friends and neighbors in Springfield, Illinois. "My friends," he began,

> No one, not in my situation, can appreciate my feeling of sadness, at this parting—To this place, and the kindness of these people, I owe every thing—Here I have been a quarter of a century, and have passed from a young to an old man. Here my children have been born, and one is buried. I now leave, not knowing when, or whether ever, I may return, with atask before me greater than that which rested upon Washington. Without the assistance of that Divine Being, who ever attended him, I cannot succeed. With that assistance I cannot fail. Trusting in Him, who can go with me, and remain with you and be everywhere for good, let us confidently hope that all will yet be well—To His care I commend you, as I hope in your prayers you will commend me, I bid you an affectionate farewell.

The president-elect and his seventeen-year-old son, Robert, then began a twelve-day journey to Washington, D.C. Concerned about his family's safety, Lincoln had his wife and their other sons, Willie and Tad, travel on another train. They joined him the next day.

Though he was greeted warmly in many northern towns and cities, Lincoln later had to cope with the sight of ugly effigies. As they approached Washington, a detective, Allan Pinkerton, learned that a band of "plug uglies" planned to sabotage bridges outside of Baltimore to stop the train and kidnap the president-elect. Consequently, Lincoln took an unmarked train to ensure that he made it to Washington safely.

Photograph of the Lincoln family home, Springfield, Illinois, 1860. (The Gilder Lehrman Collection, GLC 1262)

The Political
Quadrille cartoon

1860

A parody on the 1860 election, this cartoon highlights the impact of the Dred Scott decision on the race. Four presidential candidates dance with members of their constituency to a tune played by Dred Scott. On the top left, Breckinridge dances with Buchanan, a "goat"; on the top right, Lincoln dances with a black woman; on the bottom left, Douglas dances with an Irish immigrant; on the bottom right, Bell dances with an American Indian.

"The Political Quadrille. Music by Dred Scott," 1860. (Library of Congress Prints and Photographs Division)

SECTION IV

★

Lincoln's Presidency

Lincoln's Presidency

*by Gabor S. Boritt,
Director of the
Civil War Institute
and Fluher Professor,
Gettysburg College*

Every presidential election is important in determining the direction the United States will take, but probably none have been as important as those of 1860 and 1864. The first directly led to the greatest war in American history. The second, with Lincoln again victorious, saved the United States in body and spirit. Had his opponent, George McClellan, won, almost certainly the country would have disappeared, balkanized into hostile sections, and slavery would have continued.

Four months separated Lincoln's election to the presidency and his inauguration. During this period, there were two major compromise efforts. Compromise failed in early 1861 because it would have required the Republican party to repudiate its guiding principle: no extension of slavery into the western territories.

Why did President Lincoln refuse to allow the Confederate states to secede from the Union? Why was he unwilling to accept the argument of newspaper editor Horace Greeley that he should let the "erring sisters" depart in peace? For Lincoln, the answer was simple and straightforward. Secession was an attack on the Constitution and upon the principle of democratic self-government. The Constitution, Lincoln insisted, was a permanent compact based on the principle of majority rule. A Republican candidate won the presidency in a fair election; the Confederate states refused to accept the outcome. Even worse, the Confederate states had left the Union for the sole purpose of perpetuating slavery.

The cost of the Civil War was almost unimaginable. Its 1.5 million casualties in a nation not much over 30 million people, would with today's U.S. population of over 300 million, equal fifteen million casualties. Was the war worth it? Horrific as the cost was, few Americans from the Northern states would have said no in 1865; even fewer African Americans would have said no. Under Lincoln's leadership, the United States was saved; it was given "a new birth of freedom" with the abolition of slavery; and it was put on a road to unprecedented economic development. All this, put together, led to the great nation of today. If you wish to see Lincoln's monument, look around. It is the United States of the twenty-first century.

Many look on Lincoln as America's greatest president, and justly so. The most skillful of politicians, he appointed to his Cabinet his greatest competitors and, in the words of the Lincoln Prize–winning historian Doris Kearns Goodwin, out of this "Team of Rivals" created a solidly united team working for victory. Similarly, he forged the various factions of the North and border states into a military force that would triumph. To lead successfully, he employed his hard-earned command of the English language and a pragmatic commitment to principle combined with a bone-deep decency. He lived what he preached, the American dream of the right to rise, and because he lived it, Americans followed him.

Timeline	1861	*February 11*	Departs Springfield for Washington, D.C.
		March 4	Delivers First Inaugural Address
		April 12	Rebel forces attack Fort Sumter in Charleston, S.C. harbor; the fort surrenders a day later
		April 15	Calls for 75,000 volunteers to put down the rebellion
		April 19	Orders blockade of Confederate ports
		April 27	Authorizes the military to suspend the writ of *habeas corpus* between Philadelphia and Washington, D.C. In March 1863, Congress endorsed the suspension of *habeas corpus.*
		July 21	Union suffers a defeat at the battle of Bull Run, Va.
		August 6	First Confiscation Act, freeing slaves used by Confederates in their war effort
		September 11	Orders General John C. Fremont to modify his martial law emancipation decree
		November	Appoints General George McClellan general-in-chief of the Union army after the resignation of Lt. General Winfield Scott
			Devises compensated emancipation plan to be introduced into the Delaware state legislature
	1862	*February 20*	Son Willie dies at the age of eleven
		April 6–7	Battle of Shiloh, Tenn.
		April 16	Signs act abolishing slavery in the District of Columbia with compensation to loyal owners

May 19	Nullifies General David Hunter's martial law emancipation edict and urges the border states of Delaware, Kentucky, Maryland, and Missouri to accept gradual, compensated emancipation
June 19	Signs law barring slavery from the federal territories
July 12	Warns border state members of Congress that slavery "will be extinguished by mere friction and abrasion — by the mere incidents of the war"
July 17	Second Confiscation Act
July 22	Submits draft of Emancipation Proclamation to Cabinet
August 8	Secretary of War Edwin Stanton suspends *habeas corpus* nationwide
August 14	Lincoln's Address on Colonization to a Deputation of Free Blacks
August 29–30	Second battle of Bull Run, Va.
September 17	Union Army of the Potomac repulses Confederate offensive at the battle of Antietam, Md.
September 22	Lincoln issues Preliminary Emancipation Proclamation
November 5	Appoints Ambrose E. Burnside as commander of the Army of the Potomac, replacing George B. McClellan
December 13	Battle of Fredericksburg, Va.
1863 *January 1*	Issues Emancipation Proclamation
January 25	Appoints Joseph Hooker as commander of the Army of the Potomac, replacing Burnside

	January 29	Ulysses S. Grant is placed in command of the Army of the West, with orders to capture Vicksburg, Miss.
	March 3	Signs bill authorizing military conscription
	May 1-4	Union defeated at battle of Chancellorsville, Va.
	June 28	Appoints George G. Meade as commander of the Army of the Potomac, replacing Joseph Hooker
	July 1-3	Union defeats Confederacy at the battle of Gettysburg, Penn.
	July 4	Ulysses S. Grant's army captures Vicksburg, Miss.
	July 13-16	Draft Riots in New York City
	November 19	Delivers Gettysburg Address
1864	*March 10*	Ulysses S. Grant appointed general-in-chief of the Union army
	June 8	Renominated as the Republican party's presidential candidate
	September 2	General William Tecumseh Sherman's army captures Atlanta, Ga.
	November 8	Reelected president with 212 of 233 electoral votes and fifty-five percent of the popular vote
	December 20	General Sherman reaches Savannah, Ga., completing his "march to the sea"
1865	*January 31*	House of Representatives approves constitutional amendment abolishing slavery, and sends it to the states for ratification

March 4	Second Inaugural Address
April 9	Gen. Robert E. Lee surrenders to Gen. Ulysses S. Grant at Appomattox Court House in Virginia.

The election of Lincoln convinced Southern states that the federal government would initiate judicial and legal action against slavery. This broadside was printed in Charleston, South Carolina, on December 20, 1860, when South Carolina voted to repeal the Constitution of the United States and seceded from the Union. The Constitution of the new Confederacy would sanction the unrestricted right to hold slaves.

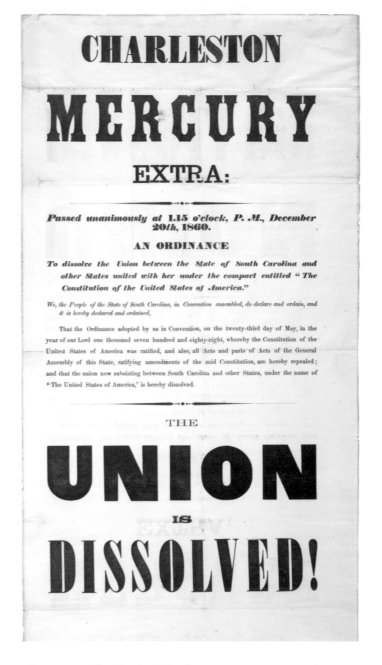

"The Union is dissolved!" [*Charleston Mercury*, Extra Ed.], December 20, 1860. (The Gilder Lehrman Collection, GLC 2688)

First
Inaugural Address

In his First Inaugural Address, the new president appealed to the "mystic chords of memory" and to "the better angels of our nature" to hold the nation together. He pledged not to interfere with slavery in the South and pleaded with the Confederate states to reconcile with the North. Twenty times he used the word "Union." But he also sent a clear signal that he would not allow the Union to be peacefully dissolved. The *Chicago Tribune* printed a special broadside, "Inaugural message of Abraham Lincoln, President of the United States," the day Lincoln was sworn into office, March 4, 1861.

Fellow-citizens of the United States:

. . . Apprehension seems to exist among the people of the Southern States, that by the accession of a Republican Administration, their property, and their peace, and personal security, are to be endangered. There has never been any reasonable cause for such apprehension. Indeed, the most ample evidence to the contrary has all the while existed, and been open to their inspection. It is found in nearly all the published speeches of him who now addresses you. I do but quote from one of those speeches when I declare that "I have no purpose, directly or indirectly, to interfere with the institution of slavery in the States where it exists. I believe I have no lawful right to do so, and I have no inclination to do so. . . ."

There is much controversy about the delivering up of fugitives from service or labor. The clause I now read is as plainly written in the Constitution as any other of its provisions:

"No person held to service or labor in one State, under the laws thereof, escaping into another, shall, in consequence of any law or regulation therein, be discharged from such service or labor, but shall be delivered up on claim of the party to whom such service or labor may be due."

It is scarcely questioned that this provision was intended by those who made it, for the reclaiming of what we call fugitive slaves; and the intention of the law-giver is the law. All members of Congress swear their support to the whole Constitution — to this provision as much as to any other. To the proposition, then, that slaves whose cases come within the terms of this clause, "shall be delivered," their oaths are unanimous. Now, if they would make the effort in good temper, could they not, with nearly equal unanimity, frame and pass a law, by means of which to keep good that unanimous oath? . . .

I hold, that in contemplation of universal law, and of the Constitution, the Union of these States is perpetual. Perpetuity is implied, if not expressed, in the fundamental law of all national governments. It is safe to assert that no government proper, ever had a provision in its organic law for its own termination. Continue to execute all the express provisions of our national Constitution, and the Union will endure forever — it being impossible to destroy it, except by some action not provided for in the instrument itself. . . .

It follows from these views that no State, upon its own mere motion, can lawfully get out of the Union, — that resolves and ordinances to that effect are legally void, and that acts of violence, within any State or States, against the authority of the United States, are insurrectionary or revolutionary, according to circumstances.

I therefore consider that in view of the Constitution and the laws, the Union is unbroken; and to the extent of my ability I shall take care, as the Constitution itself expressly enjoins upon me, that the laws of the Union be faithfully executed in all the States. . . .

In doing this there needs to be no bloodshed or violence, and there shall be none unless it be forced upon the national authority. The power confided to me will be used to hold, occupy, and possess the property and places belonging to the Government and to collect the duties and imposts; but beyond what may be necessary for these objects, there will be no invasion, no using of force against or among the people anywhere. Where hostility to the United States in any interior locality shall be so great and universal as to prevent competent resident citizens from holding the Federal offices, there will be no attempt to force obnoxious strangers among the people for that object. While the strict legal right may exist in the Government to enforce the exercise of these offices, the attempt to do so would be so irritating and so nearly impracticable withal that I deem it better to forego for the time the uses of such offices. . . .

Plainly, the central idea of secession, is the essence of anarchy. A majority, held in restraint by constitutional checks and limitations, and always changing easily with deliberate changes of popular opinions and sentiments, is the only true sovereign of a free people. . . . One section of our country believes slavery is right, and ought to be extended, while the other believes it is wrong, and ought not to be extended. This is the only substantial dispute. . . . Physically speaking, we cannot separate. We can not remove our respective sections from each other, nor build an impassable wall between them. . . .

In your hands, my dissatisfied fellow countrymen, and not in mine, is the momentous issue of civil war. The government will not assail you. You can have no conflict without being yourselves the aggressors. You have no oath registered in Heaven to destroy the government, while I shall have the most solemn one to "preserve, protect, and defend it."

I am loath to close. We are not enemies, but friends. We must not be enemies. Though passion may have strained, it must not break our bonds of affection. The mystic chords of memory, stretching from every battle-field, and patriot grave, to every living heart and hearth-stone, all over this broad land, will yet swell the chorus of the Union, when again touched, as surely they will be, by the better angels of our nature.

Photograph of Mary Todd Lincoln in her Inaugural Ball gown, 1861. (The Gilder Lehrman Collection, GLC 5111.02.0052)

Fort Sumter: Conflict Commences

When he delivered his First Inaugural Address, Lincoln assumed that there was time for pro-union sentiment among southerners, which he greatly overestimated, to reassert itself, making a peaceful resolution to the crisis possible. The next morning, however, he received a letter from Major Robert Anderson, commander of the federal forces manning Fort Sumter, an installation guarding Charleston, South Carolina's harbor. Anderson informed the president that Fort Sumter's supplies would be exhausted in four to six weeks and that it would take 20,000 troops to reinforce the fort.

Lincoln decided to try to re-supply the fort with provisions peacefully using unarmed ships and to inform the Confederate government of his decision beforehand. Only if the South Carolinians used force to stop the mission would warships, positioned outside Charleston harbor, go into action. In this way, Lincoln hoped to make the Confederacy responsible for starting a war, should one break out. He wished to prolong the status quo without provoking war and to give southern Unionists the opportunity to recapture control of the seceding states. Upon learning of Lincoln's plan, the newly inaugurated president of the Confederacy, Jefferson Davis, ordered General Pierre G.T. Beauregard to force Fort Sumter's surrender before the supply mission could arrive. At 4:30 a.m. on April 12, guns began firing on Fort Sumter. Thirty-three hours later, the installation surrendered. Astonishingly, there were no fatalities on either side during the clash.

On April 13, 1861, the *Marietta (Ohio) Home News* published an extra edition which contained a detailed account of the events that took place leading up to and during the attack on Fort Sumter.

Keep Curios

Marietta Ohio

(1861)

HOME NEWS EXTRA, APR. 13, 11 P.M.

TERRIBLE NEWS!
THE FIGHT RAGES!
FORT SUMTER ON FIRE!
Washington in Danger!
SURRENDER OF FORT SUMTER!
REBEL VICTORY!

The Fleet to Enter the Harbor.

NEW YORK, April 13.

The opinion prevails that an attempt will be made before sunrise to run the light draught vessels of the fleet up to Fort Sumter to reenforce Major Anderson and also supply him with provisions.

The Battle Still Raging.

CHARLESTON, April 13.

The cannonading is going on fiercely from all points, from the vessels outside and all along the coast.

It is reported that Fort Sumter is on fire.

Fort Sumter on Fire!

CHARLESTON, April 13—1 P.M.

The roof of Fort Sumter is in a sheet of blaze. Major Anderson has ceased firing to extinguish it. Two of his magazines have exploded. The shells are flying over and around Fort Sumter in quick succession. The war vessels cannot get in on account of the ebbing tide. They are at anchor. Fort Moultrie appears to be considerably disabled. The Federal flag still waves over Fort Sumter.

Anderson's Shells fly Thick and Fast.

CHARLESTON, April 13—10 A.M.

At intervals of twenty minutes the firing was kept up all night on Fort Sumter. Major Anderson's strongest shells fly thick and fast, and they can be seen in their course from the Charleston City Battery.

SAVANNAH, April 13.

The lights at Tybee and in this harbor have been discontinued for the present.

How Lincoln Received the News.

WASHINGTON, April 13.

Commander Fox, spoken of in the Charleston dispatches, commands the vessel with provisions which was to lead the expedition into Charleston.

The President received the war news calmly.

The Merrimack Getting Ready.

NORFOLK, April 13.

Orders have been received to fit up the frigate Merrimack immediately.

The War News in Boston.

BOSTON, April 13.

The war news from Charleston creates a profound sensation in this city and throughout the State. The general sentiment is that the Federal Government is right and shall be sustained.

The Traitor Tyler at Richmond.

RICHMOND, VA., April 13.

Hon. John Tyler received this morning from Montgomery copies of the official dispatches between Gen. Beauregard and Maj. Anderson and Secretary of War Walker. They were printed and circulated through the country.

Rhode Island Offers Troops.

PROVIDENCE, April 13.

Gov. Sprague has tendered the Government the service of the Marine Armory and 1000 Infantry, and offers to accompany them himself.

Army Officers Removed.

WASHINGTON, April 13.

The President has directed that Capt. W. B. St. John, 3d Infantry, and Lieut. Abner Smead, 1st Artillery, cease to be officers of the army. The regular troops here have been ordered to proceed to the outskirts of the city to watch every avenue thereto, while the Volunteers guard the Armory and public buildings. Videttes are constantly seen riding through the streets. There is comparatively but little excitement here relative to affairs in Charleston.

The Confederate Flag to Wave Over the Frderal Capitol!

MONTGOMERY, April 13.

The President and Secretary of War were serenaded last night. The latter was called out. He said the Confederate flag would soon be waving over Fort Sumter and from the Federal Capitol.

Good News from Texas.

NEW YORK, April 13.

Dispatches from Col. Wade, commander of the Texan forces states that a strong Union feeling is growing.

Gov. Houston predicts the return of the secessionists to their allegiance, they are terribly taxed. Houston has been offered armed support by the Mormons in every part of the State.

Sumter in Distress!

CHARLESTON, April 13, 4 P.M.

The flag on Fort Sumter is at half mast—signal of distress.

Sumter Shows the White Flag!

CAARLESTON, April 13, 6 P.M.

The White Flag was raised, and Fort Sumter surrendered this evening.

News of the Confederate attack on Fort Sumter, South Carolina, *Marietta (Ohio) Home News*, April 13, 1861. (The Gilder Lehrman Collection, GLC 1540.06)

Lincoln and Civil Liberties

During the Civil War, President Lincoln received heated criticism, mainly from Democrats, for violating civil liberties. He was denounced for imposing martial law, closing newspapers, using military tribunals to try civilians, jailing editors, and holding thousands of Democrats opposed to the war in military prisons.

Lincoln endured the greatest criticism of his presidency for suspending the writ of *habeas corpus*, the right of detained persons to have a civil court determine whether they are imprisoned lawfully, in Maryland and parts of the Midwest. He did this partly in response to threats of secession in Maryland, and to safeguard the movement of Union troops to Washington, D.C. Lincoln also hoped to quell rioting and violence in southern Indiana and elsewhere. In the fall of 1862, the president extended the suspension of *habeas corpus* to the entire nation, to prevent obstruction of the military draft. Though the Constitution gave the government the power to suspend the writ "in Cases of Rebellion," many critics insisted only Congress could do so. Lincoln acted alone to suspend the writ, he said, because Congress was not in session and the emergency required action.

In this letter to Secretary of War Edwin Stanton, Lincoln revokes General Ambrose Burnside's notorious General Order 84, which barred the circulation of the *Chicago Times* within the Department of the Ohio. Burnside was infuriated by the *Chicago Times* for its criticism of his treatment of Clement Vallandigham, leader of the Peace Democrats. On May 5, 1863, Burnside had arrested Vallandigham. Vallandigham was charged with publicly expressing "sympathies for those in arms against the Government of the United States." He was tried by court-martial, found guilty and sentenced to prison for the remainder of the war.

Lincoln was embarrassed by the Vallandigham affair, which he learned about from the newspapers. He was also aware of the negative political ramifications of Order 84, which was widely denounced. As a way of limiting the damage, Lincoln reduced Vallandigham's punishment from imprisonment to exile in the South, and revoked Burnside's order.

In May 1863, a Democratic Convention in Albany, New York, voted to censure the Lincoln administration for acts that it considered unconstitutional, including the arbitrary arrest of civilians in the North. In a letter written in June 1863, addressed to Erastus Corning and others, Lincoln responded to the charge that he was subverting the Constitution, arguing that acts that might be illegal in time of peace may be necessary "in cases of rebellion" when the nation's survival was at stake.

Abraham Lincoln to Edwin M. Stanton

June 4, 1863

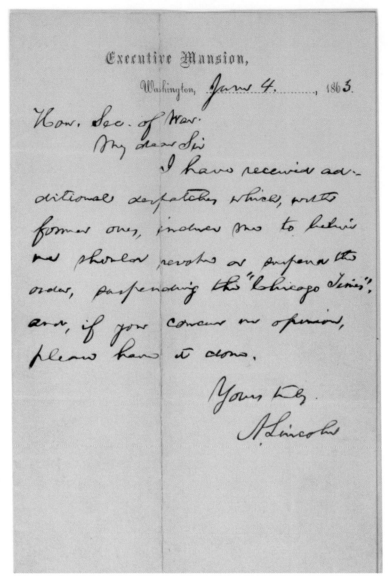

Letter from Abraham Lincoln to Edwin M. Stanton, June 4, 1863.
(The Gilder Lehrman Collection, GLC 1)

Executive Mansion

Washington, June 4. 1863.

Hon. Sec. of War.

    My dear Sir

        I have received additional dispatches which, with former ones, induce me to believe we should revoke or suspend the order, suspending the "Chicago Times", and, if you concur in opinion, please have it done.

Yours truly

A. Lincoln

Abraham Lincoln to Erastus Corning and others, June 12, 1863.
(Robert Todd Lincoln Collection, Library of Congress)

I understand the meeting, whose resolutions I am considering, to be in favor of suppressing the rebellion by military force — by armies. Long experience has shown that armies can not be maintained unless desertion shall be punished by the severe penalty of death. The case requires, and the law and the constitution, sanction this punishment. Must I shoot a simple-minded soldier boy who deserts, while I must not touch a hair of a wiley agitator who induces him to desert? This is none the less injurious when effected by getting a father, or brother, or friend, into a public meeting, and there working upon his feeling, till he is persuaded to write the soldier boy, that he is fighting in a bad cause, for a wicked administration of a contemptable government, too weak to arrest and punish him if he shall desert. I think that in such a case, to silence the agitator, and save the boy, is not only constitutional, but, withal, a great mercy.

Lincoln as Commander in Chief

Acknowledging his limited military training, Lincoln became a "self-taught military expert." He studied and read books on military history that he borrowed from the Library of Congress and became deeply committed to learning from their accounts. The following letters suggest the active role President Lincoln, as commander in chief, played in monitoring the day-to-day events and formulating a military strategy for the Union army.

Abraham Lincoln to Charles H. Russell

May 16, 1861

Washington D.C.

May 16. 1861

C. H. Russell, Esq.

My dear Sir:

Learning today from Gov. Seward that the order you have for forwarding the fourteen Regiments has something in it for the Governor to do in this case, I am alarmed lest a <u>see-sawing</u> commences, by which neither your troops nor the Governor's will get along in any reasonable time. Now, I want you to cut the Knots, and send them right along — five Regiments here, and nine to Fort Sumpter, just as understood when we parted.

Yours very truly

A. Lincoln

Private

Washington D.C.
May 16. 1861

C. H. Russell, Esq
My dear Sir:
Learning to-day from
Gov. Seward that the order you
have for forwarding the fourteen
Regiments has something in it
for the Governor to do in the
case, I am alarmed lest a
see—sawing commences, by which
neither your troops nor the Governor's will get along in any
reasonable time— Now, I want
you to cut the knots, and
send them right along—
five Regiments here, and new
to Fort-Sumter, just as ordered-
town when we parted—
Yours very truly
A. Lincoln

Letter from Abraham Lincoln to Charles H. Russell, May 16, 1861. (The Gilder Lehrman Collection, GLC 635)

Abraham Lincoln to Edwin M. Stanton

May 20, 1862

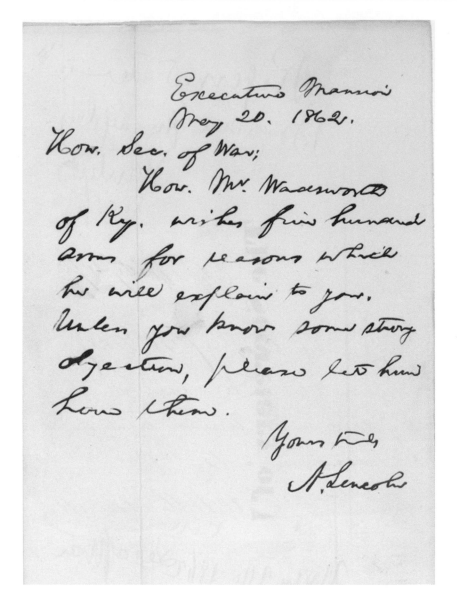

Letter from Abraham Lincoln to Edwin M. Stanton, May 20, 1862. (The Gilder Lehrman Collection, GLC 746)

Executive Mansion
May 20. 1862.

Hon. Sec. of War,

Hon. Mr. Wadsworth of Ky. wishes five hundred arms for reasons which he will explain to you. Unless you know some strong objection, please let him have them.

Yours truly
A. Lincoln

*Abraham Lincoln
to Daniel Butterfield*

May 3, 1863

Letter from Abraham Lincoln to Daniel Butterfield, May 3, 1863. (The Gilder Lehrman Collection, GLC5977)

> Washington City.
> May 3. 1863
>
> Major General Butterfield.
>
> Where is Gen. Hooker? Where is Sedgwick? Where is Stoneman?
>
> A. Lincoln.

The battle of Antietam in Maryland, on September 17, 1862, was the bloodiest single day of the Civil War. Lee's Confederate army suffered 11,000 casualties; McClellan's Union forces lost 13,000. Lee was forced to retreat, allowing the North to declare the battle a Union victory. But Union forces under the command of McClellan failed to follow up on their surprise success and defeat Lee's army.

In the following exchange, Lincoln expresses anger over the statement of one officer, Major John J. Key, whose brother was a McClellan staff officer. According to Key, it was not the objective of the war to crush the Confederate army. Instead, Key implied, the goal was simply to drag the war out until both sides gave up and the Union could be restored with slavery intact. Key was the only officer dismissed from service for uttering disloyal sentiments. However, Lincoln was suspicious that many others, even up to General McClellan, were reluctant to wage war too rigorously against slavery. McClellan was relieved of command in November 1862, and many of his officers were re-assigned.

Here, Lincoln delivers an uncharacteristically harsh punishment. The letter portrays Lincoln as an active commander in chief taking personal interest in the disloyalty charges against Major John J. Key.

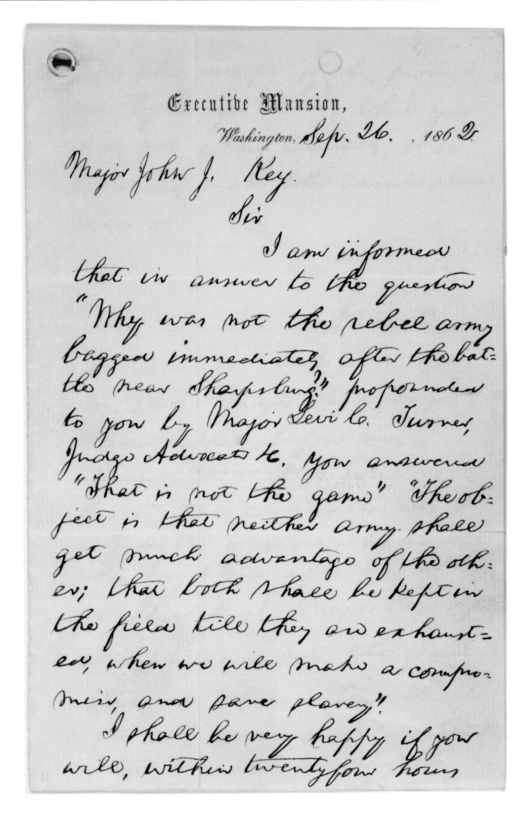

Letter from Abraham Lincoln to John J. Key, September 26, 1862. Page 1. (The Gilder Lehrman Collection, GLC 228)

from the receipt of this, prove to
me by Major Turner, that you
did not, either literally, or in
substance, make the answer stated—

Yours

A. Lincoln

At about 11 o'clock A.m. Sep.
27. 1862. Major Key & Major
Turner appear before me.
Major Turner says, "As I remember it, the conversation was, I
asked the question why we did
not bag them after the battle
at Sharpsburg? Major Key's reply
was that was not the game.
that we should tire them selv-
es out and ourselves, that
that was the only way th

Letter from Abraham Lincoln to John J. Key, September 26, 1862. Page 2. (The Gilder Lehrman Collection, GLC228)

Abraham Lincoln
to Major John J. Key

September 16, 1862

Executive Mansion,

Washington, Sep. 26. 1862.

Major John J. Key.

Sir

I am informed that in answer to the question "Why was not the rebel army bagged immediately after the battle near Sharpsburg?" propounded to you by Major Levi C. Turner, Judge Advocate &c. you answered "That is not the game" "The object is that neither army shall get much advantage of the other; that both shall be kept in the field till they are exhausted, when we will make a compromise, and save slavery".

I shall be very happy if you will, within twentyfour hours from the receipt of this, prove to me by Major Turner, that you did not, either literally, or in substance, make the answer stated.

Yours

A. Lincoln

[Lincoln recounted his interview with Major Key on September 27, 1862:]

At about 11 o'clock AM. Sep. 27. 1862 Major Key & Major Turner appear before me. Major Turner says, "As I remember it, the conversation was, I asked the question why we did not bag them after the battle at Sharpsburg? Major Key's reply was that was not the game, that we should tire the rebels out and ourselves; that that was the only way the Union could be preserved, we come together fraternally, and slavery be saved."

On cross-examination Major Turner says he has frequently heard Major Key converse, in regard to the present troubles, and never heard him utter a sentiment unfavorable to the maintenance of the Union. He has never uttered anything which he Maj. T would call disloyalty. . . .

[After the interview, Lincoln wrote:]

In my view it is wholly inadmissable for any gentleman holding a military commission from the United States to utter such sentiments as Major Key is within proven to have done. Therefore let Major John J. Key, be forthwith dismissed from the Military service of the United States.

The Gettysburg Address

In a bid to shatter northern morale and win European recognition for the Confederacy, Lee's army launched a daring invasion of Pennsylvania in mid-1863. On July 1, 1863, a Confederate brigade ran into Union cavalry near Gettysburg, and the largest battle ever fought in the western hemisphere broke out.

After Gettysburg, Lee was never able to mount another major offensive. There were fifty thousand casualties at the battle of Gettysburg. A quarter of the Union forces and a third of the Confederates were killed, wounded, captured, or missing. The government subsequently paid $1.59 a corpse to have the bodies buried.

On November 19, 1863, four months after the battle, a ceremony was held to dedicate a cemetery for the Union dead. The main speaker was Edward Everett, a former U.S. Senator, governor of Massachusetts, and president of Harvard. Everett spoke for two hours, recounting the battle of Gettysburg in vivid detail.

President Lincoln had been invited to make a "few appropriate remarks" at the cemetery's consecration. Some 15,000 people heard his remarks. Less than 275 words in length, Lincoln's three-minute-long Gettysburg address defined the meaning of the Civil War.

Drawing upon the biblical concepts of suffering, consecration, and resurrection, he described the war as a momentous chapter in the global struggle for self-government, liberty, and equality.

Seven times in his brief speech, Lincoln referred to the United States as a single nation bound together by a common set of values, above all a commitment to "the proposition that all men are created equal." In so stating Lincoln drew a clear line back to Jefferson's words in the Declaration of Independence.

Four score and seven years ago our fathers brought forth, on this continent, a new nation, conceived in Liberty, and dedicated to the proposition that all men are created equal.

Now we are engaged in a great civil war, testing whether that nation, or any nation so conceived, and so dedicated, can long endure. We are met on a great battle-field of that war. We have come to dedicate a portion of that field, as a final resting-place for those who here gave their lives, that that nation might live. It is altogether fitting and proper that we should do this.

But, in a larger sense, we can not dedicate— we can not consecrate— we can not hallow— this ground. The brave men, living and dead, who struggled here, have consecrated it, far above our poor power to add or detract. The world will little note, nor long remember what we say here, but it can never forget what they did here. It is for us the living, rather, to be dedicated here to the unfinished work which they who fought here have thus far so nobly advanced. It is rather for us to be here dedicated to the great task remaining be-

The Gettysburg Address, delivered by Abraham Lincoln, November 19, 1863. Page 1. (Courtesy of the Division of Rare and Manuscript Collections, Cornell University Library)

fore us— that from these honored dead we take increased devotion to that cause for which they here gave the last full measure of devotion— that we here highly resolve that these dead shall not have died in vain— that this nation, under God, shall have a new birth of freedom— and that government of the people, by the people, for the people, shall not perish from the earth.

The Gettysburg Address, delivered by Abraham Lincoln, November 19, 1863. Page 2. (Courtesy of the Division of Rare and Manuscript Collections, Cornell University Library)

Abraham Lincoln,
The Gettysburg
Address

November 19, 1863

Four score and seven years ago our fathers brought forth, on this continent, a new nation, conceived in Liberty, and dedicated to the proposition that all men are created equal.

Now we are engaged in a great civil war, testing whether that nation, or any nation so conceived, and so dedicated, can long endure. We are met on a great battle-field of that war. We have come to dedicate a portion of that field, as a final resting-place for those who here gave their lives, that that nation might live. It is altogether fitting and proper that we should do this.

But, in a larger sense, we can not dedicate — we can not consecrate — we can not hallow — this ground. The brave men, living and dead, who struggled here, have consecrated it far above our poor power to add or detract. The world will little note, nor long remember what we say here, but it can never forget what they did here. It is for us the living, rather, to be dedicated here to the unfinished work which they who fought here have thus far so nobly advanced. It is rather for us to be here dedicated to the great task remaining before us — that from these honored dead we take increased devotion to that cause for which they here gave the last full measure of devotion — that we here highly resolve that these dead shall not have died in vain — that this nation, under God, shall have a new birth of freedom — and that government of the people, by the people, for the people, shall not perish from the earth.

SECTION V

Lincoln and Race

Lincoln and Race

*by David W. Blight,
Class of 1954
Professor of American
History, Yale University*

One of the most fascinating and important aspects of Abraham Lincoln's thought and character was his capacity to change and grow. Nothing illustrates this any better than his evolving ideas on slavery and emancipation, especially in the pivotal war years. There is no question that Lincoln always hated slavery and wished it eliminated, for the good of black people and for the fate of the American republic. Lincoln had both personal prejudice and political reticence to overcome on the issue of race, the greatest test of his presidential and moral leadership. He denounced social equality between the races in the debates with Stephen Douglas in 1858; accepted an aborted first version of a Thirteenth Amendment in 1861 that would have guaranteed the right of slave ownership in the existing slave states; and made an insensitive statement to a black delegation at the White House in August 1862, urging that whites and blacks "should be separated," and that the best hope for blacks lay in foreign colonization.

But as the scale of the war broadened, as the aims of Union victory escalated to the conquest of Southern society, Lincoln came to see the destruction of slavery as part and parcel of saving and, in turn, reinventing the American nation. A combination of Lincoln's own humane proclivities, the necessities of a totalizing war, his personal capacity for intellectual and moral growth, and the will of slaves themselves to be free made the president a "great emancipator." Lincoln's legalistic blueprint for black freedom spelled out in the Emancipation Proclamation, his subtle but forceful defense of that action in the Conkling letter, and his enduring declaration in the Second Inaugural Address that "all knew" that "somehow" slavery was the "cause of the war" demonstrate that once he had decided for abolition, he never turned his back on this great aim. In the last months of the war Lincoln worked forcefully for the passage of the ultimate Thirteenth Amendment, desiring Constitutional authority behind his executive order because he feared that in the wake of the war ex-slaveholders might sue endlessly in court for compensation or restitution for their millions of dollars worth of "property."

Timeline	1861	*September 11*	Orders General John C. Fremont to modify his emancipation decree
	1862	*April 16*	Signs act abolishing slavery in the District of Columbia with compensation to loyal owners
		May 19	Nullifies General Hunter's martial law emancipation edict and urges the border states of Delaware, Kentucky, Maryland, and Missouri to accept gradual, compensated emancipation
		June 19	Signs law barring slavery from the federal territories
		July 12	Warns border state members of Congress that slavery "will be extinguished by mere friction and abrasion—by the mere incidents of the war"
		August 14	Lincoln's Address on Colonization to a Deputation of Free Blacks
		September 22	Issues Preliminary Emancipation Proclamation
	1863	*January 1*	Issues Emancipation Proclamation

*Debate with
Stephen Douglas at
Ottawa, Illinois*

Lincoln was not a radical abolitionist. Unlike William Lloyd Garrison or Frederick Douglass, he favored a gradualist approach to emancipation that would provide compensation to slave owners. As late as 1863, he still envisioned various schemes to colonize blacks abroad.

Nor was he a racial egalitarian. As a member of the Illinois state legislature, he failed to oppose state laws which required any black entering the state to post a $1,000 bond and prohibited African Americans from voting, serving on juries, holding office, and intermarrying with whites. During his debate with Stephen Douglas in Ottawa, a pro-slavery part of the state, Lincoln insisted that he opposed introducing "political and social equality between the white and black races."

POLITICAL DEBATES

BETWEEN

HON. ABRAHAM LINCOLN

AND

HON. STEPHEN A. DOUGLAS,

In the Celebrated Campaign of 1858, in Illinois;

INCLUDING THE PRECEDING SPEECHES OF EACH, AT CHI-
CAGO, SPRINGFIELD, ETC.; ALSO, THE TWO GREAT
SPEECHES OF MR. LINCOLN IN OHIO, IN 1859,

AS

CAREFULLY PREPARED BY THE REPORTERS OF EACH PARTY, AND PUBLISHED
AT THE TIMES OF THEIR DELIVERY.

COLUMBUS:
FOLLETT, FOSTER AND COMPANY.
1860.

Title page of an 1860 book reprinting political debates between Abraham Lincoln and Stephen A. Douglas in the 1858 Senate campaign. (The Gilder Lehrman Collection. GLC 2957)

I have no purpose to introduce political and social equality between the white and the black races. There is a physical difference between the two, which in my judgment will probably forever forbid their living together upon the footing of perfect equality, and inasmuch as it becomes a necessity that there must be a difference, I, as well as Judge Douglas, am in favor of the race to which I belong, having the superior position. I have never said anything to the contrary, but I hold that notwithstanding all this, there is no reason in the world why the negro is not entitled to all the natural rights enumerated in the Declaration of Independence, the right to life, liberty and the pursuit of happiness. [Loud cheers.] I hold that he is as much entitled to these as the white man. I agree with Judge Douglas he is not my equal in many respects — certainly not in color, perhaps not in moral or intellectual endowment. But in the right to eat the bread, without leave of anybody else, which his own hand earns, *he is my equal and the equal of Judge Douglas, and the equal of every living man.*

A Proposed Thirteenth Amendment to Protect Slavery

Two weeks after taking the oath of office, President Lincoln sent copies of a proposed Thirteenth Amendment to the U.S. Constitution to each state governor. President James Buchanan had called on Congress to draft an "explanatory" amendment to reassure the South that a Republican president would not threaten slavery. In a last ditch effort to save the Union, a Republican member of Congress, Thomas Corwin of Ohio, drafted an amendment that would permanently bar the federal government from interfering with slavery in the states where it existed. The amendment passed the House on February 28, 1861, and the Senate on March 2, two days before Lincoln's inauguration. The amendment read:

> No amendment shall be made to the Constitution which will authorize or give to Congress the power to abolish or interfere, within any State, with the domestic institutions thereof, including that of persons held to labor or service by the laws of said State.

In his First Inaugural Address, Lincoln had expressed his support for an amendment which would make "express and irrevocable" the principle that "the federal government, shall never interfere with the domestic institutions of the States, including that of persons held to service." In the end, the only states to ratify the proposed amendment were Maryland and Ohio.

To His Excellency,

The Governor of the State of California,
Sacramento.

Washington, March 16, 1861.

Sir:

I transmit an authenticated copy of a Joint Resolution to amend the Constitution of the United States, adopted by Congress and approved on the 2d of March, 1861, by James Buchanan, President.

I have the honor to be,

Your Excellency's obedient servant,

Abraham Lincoln

By the President:

Willi... H. Sew...
Secretary of State.

Official document signed by Abraham Lincoln to the governor of California, transmitting a proposed Constitutional amendment, March 16, 1861. (The Gilder Lehrman Collection, GLC 5631)

Nathaniel Gordon Case

Abraham Lincoln's lifelong hatred of slavery is demonstrated in his refusal to commute slave trader Nathaniel Gordon's sentence of execution. This stunning document stands out in the papers of Lincoln, a man renowned for his mercy and willingness to pardon. That Lincoln granted Nathaniel Gordon a "respite" from execution, but not clemency, is a testament to his growing public intolerance for slavery. Gordon is believed to be the only man to be executed by the U.S. for participating in the slave trade.

Lincoln's compassionate nature is not completely deaf to Gordon's pleas for mercy. Acknowledging that Gordon may not have had ample time to reconcile himself to his fate, Lincoln grants the prisoner a two-week respite to prepare himself for death and urges Gordon to make his peace with God. More remarkably, Lincoln bears full responsibility for ending this man's life and painstakingly orders the time and the date that the execution will occur.

In the case of Nathaniel Gordon, Lincoln reaffirmed his opposition to slavery and placed the prisoner beyond the reach of mercy, making an example of Gordon to all slave traders, to the Confederacy, and to Great Britain. Gordon's execution preceded a series of anti-slavery measures including the abolition of slavery in Washington, D.C., and a new treaty with Great Britain to more effectively halt the transatlantic slave trade. The acts culminated in the Emancipation Proclamation.

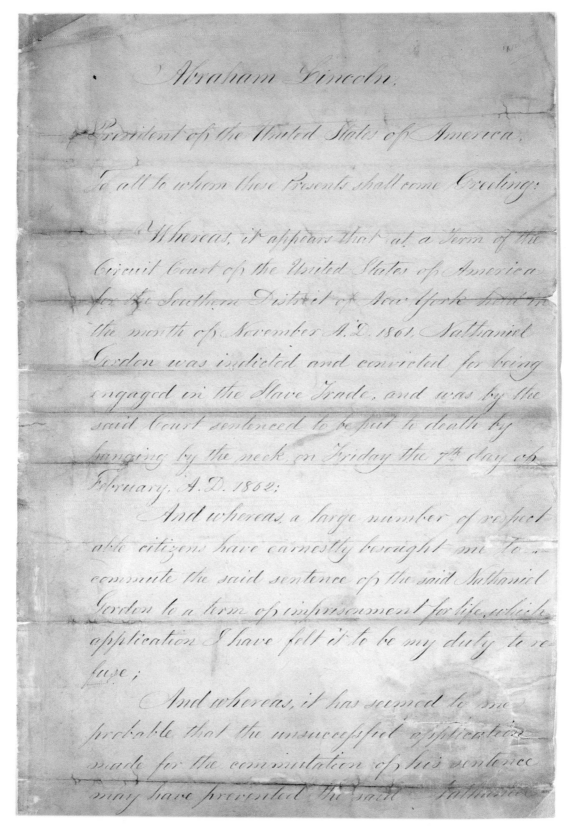

Abraham Lincoln,

President of the United States of America,

To all to whom these Presents shall come Greeting:

Whereas, it appears that at a Term of the Circuit Court of the United States of America for the Southern District of New York held in the month of November A.D. 1861, Nathaniel Gordon was indicted and convicted for being engaged in the Slave Trade, and was by the said Court sentenced to be put to death by hanging by the neck, on Friday the 7th day of February, A.D. 1862:

And whereas, a large number of respectable citizens have earnestly besought me to commute the said sentence of the said Nathaniel Gordon to a term of imprisonment for life, which application I have felt it to be my duty to refuse;

And whereas, it has seemed to me probable that the unsuccessful application made for the commutation of his sentence may have prevented the said Nathaniel

Abraham Lincoln's decision in the Nathaniel Gordon case, February 4, 1862. Page 1. (The Gilder Lehrman Collection, GLC 182)

Gordon from making the necessary preparation for the awful change which awaits him;

Now, therefore, be it known, that I, Abraham Lincoln, President of the United States of America, have granted and do hereby grant unto him, the said Nathaniel Gordon, a respite of the above recited sentence, until Friday the twenty-first day of February, A.D. 1862, between the hours of twelve o'clock at noon and three o'clock in the afternoon of the said day, when the said sentence shall be executed.

In granting this respite it becomes my painful duty to admonish the prisoner that, relinquishing all expectation of pardon by Human Authority, he refer himself alone to the mercy of the common God and Father of all men.

In testimony whereof, I have hereunto signed my name and caused the Seal of the United States to be affixed.

Done at the City of Washington,

Abraham Lincoln's decision in the Nathaniel Gordon case, February 4, 1862. Page 2. (The Gilder Lehrman Collection, GLC 182)

Abraham Lincoln
President of the United States of America.

To all to whom these Presents shall come Greeting:

Whereas, it appears that at a Term of the Circuit Court of the United States of America for the Southern District of New York held in the month of November A.D. 1861, Nathaniel Gordon was indicted and convicted for being engaged in the Slave Trade, and was by the said Court sentenced to be put to death by hanging by the neck, on Friday the 7th day of February, A.D. 1862;

And whereas, a large number of respectable citizens have earnestly besought me to commute the said sentence of the said Nathaniel Gordon to a term of imprisonment for life, which application I have felt it to be my duty to refuse;

And whereas, it has seemed to me probable that the unsuccessful application made for the commutation of his sentence may have prevented the said Nathaniel Gordon from making the necessary preparation for the awful change which awaits him;

Now, therefore, be it known, that I, Abraham Lincoln, President of the United States of America have granted and do hereby grant unto him, the said Nathaniel Gordon, a respite of the above recited sentence, until Friday the twenty first day of February, A.D. 1862, between the hours of twelve o'clock at noon and three o'clock in the afternoon of the said day when the said sentence shall be executed.

In granting this respite, it becomes my painful duty to admonish the prisoner that, relinquishing all expectation of pardon by Human Authority, he refer himself alone to the mercy of the Common God and Father of all men.

In testimony whereof, I have hereunto signed my name and caused the Seal of the United States to be affixed. Done at the City of Washington this Fourth day of February A.D. 1862, and of the Independence of the United States the Eighty sixth.

Abraham Lincoln

By the President

William H. Seward
Secretary of State

Separation of Races

For much of his political career, Lincoln, like his political idol Henry Clay, was an advocate of colonization. In 1862, the president met with a group of African Americans at the White House (no previous president had dreamed of inviting blacks to the White House) and, in what was perhaps the lowest point of his presidency, seemed to blame blacks for the Civil War. In the preceding months, at President Lincoln's urging, Congress had appropriated $600,000 that the president could use to colonize blacks outside the United States.

Frederick Douglass condemned Lincoln's remarks. "No sincere wish to improve the condition of the oppressed has dictated" his words, Douglass wrote. "It expresses merely the desire to get rid of them, and reminds one of the politeness with which a man might try to bow out of his house some troublesome creditor or the witness of some old guilt."

On December 31, 1862, one day before the Emancipation Proclamation took effect, President Lincoln authorized the establishment of a colony for former slaves on the Island of Vache, 12 miles off the coast of Haiti. By the beginning of June 1863, 453 former slaves had been transported to the colony. Small pox and mismanagement by a white government-appointed manager contributed to the colony's failure. The transport ship dispatched by President Lincoln at the beginning of 1864 picked up only 368 survivors.

Address on Colonization to a Deputation of Free Blacks

August 14, 1862

Having all been seated, the President . . . informed them that a sum of money had been appropriated by Congress, and placed at his disposition for the purpose of aiding the colonization in some country of the people, or a portion of them, of African descent . . . Why, he asked, should the people of your race be colonized, and where? Why should they leave this country? . . . You and we are different races. We have between us a broader difference than exists between almost any other two races. Whether it is right or wrong I need not discuss, but this physical difference is a great disadvantage to us both, as I think your race suffer very greatly, many of them by living among us, while ours suffer from your presence. In a word we suffer on each side. If this is admitted, it affords a reason at least why we should be separated.

Your race are suffering, in my judgment, the greatest wrong inflicted on any people. But even when you cease to be slaves, you are yet far removed from being placed on an equality with the white race. You are cut off from many of the advantages which the other race enjoy. The aspiration of men is to enjoy equality with the best when free, but on this broad continent, not a single man of your race is made the equal of a single man of ours. Go where you are treated the best, and the ban is still upon you.

I do not propose to discuss this, but to present it as a fact with which we have to deal. . . . I need not recount to you the effects upon white men, growing out of the institution of Slavery. I believe in its general evil effects on the white race. See our present condition—the country engaged in war!—our white men cutting one another's throats, none knowing how far it will extend. . . . But for your race among us there could not be war, although many men engaged on either side do not care for you one way or the other. Nevertheless, I repeat, without the institution of Slavery and the colored race as a basis, the war could not have an existence.

It is better for us both, therefore, to be separated. I know that there are free men among you, who even if they could better their condition are not as much inclined to go out of the country . . . I suppose one of the principal difficulties in the way of colonization is that the free colored man cannot see that his comfort would be advanced by it. You may believe you can live in Washington or elsewhere in the United States the remainder of your life [as easily], perhaps more so than you can in any foreign country, and hence you may come to the conclusion that you have nothing to do with the idea of going to a foreign country. This is (I speak in no unkind sense) an extremely selfish view of the case.

But you ought to do something to help those who are not so fortunate as yourselves. There is an unwillingness on the part of our people, harsh as it may be, for you free colored people to remain with us. . . . If intelligent colored men, such as are before me, would move in this matter, much might be accomplished. It is exceedingly important that we have men at the beginning capable of thinking as white men, and not those who have been systematically oppressed.

Photograph of the White House with soldiers in the foreground, Washington, D.C., 1862. (The Gilder Lehrman Collection, GLC 5111.02.0039)

Even after the momentous Union victories at Gettysburg, Pa. and Vicksburg, Miss. in July 1863, many northern Democrats continued to demand an immediate end to the war, which would have allowed slavery to remain a legal institution. In a letter to a long-time friend in Springfield, Illinois, intended to be read at a mass meeting, President Lincoln defended the Emancipation Proclamation and his decision to enlist black troops, while expressing a fear that his political opponents would not reconcile themselves to black freedom.

*Excerpt from a
Letter from
Abraham Lincoln
to James C. Conkling*

August 26, 1863

Abraham Lincoln to James C. Conkling, August 26, 1863. (Robert Todd Lincoln Collection, Library of Congress)

Peace does not appear so distant as it did. I hope it will come soon, and come to stay; and so come as to be worth the keeping in all future time. It will then have been proved that, among free men, there can be no successful appeal from the ballot to the bullet; and that they who take such appeal are sure to lose their case, and pay the cost. And then, there will be some black men who can remember that, with silent tongue, and clenched teeth, and steady [*inserted*: eye], and well ~~borne~~ poised bayonet, they have helped mankind on to this great consummation; while [*inserted*: I fear], there will be some white ones, unable to forget that, with malignant heart, and deceitful speech, they have strove to hinder it.

SECTION VI

★

Lincoln and Emancipation

Lincoln and Emancipation

*by Allen C. Guelzo,
Henry R. Luce Professor
of the Civil War Era
and Professor of History,
Gettysburg College*

Lincoln insisted that "I have always hated slavery." And there was never any doubt in his own mind that preserving slavery was the one fundamental agenda of the Confederates in seceding from the Union. Nevertheless, Lincoln remained keenly aware that his position as president, no matter how powerful it seemed, gave him no authority to abolish slavery. Slavery was legalized by individual state enactments, and the federal government had no authority to interfere in those arrangements. He could, however, employ a number of indirect means to persuade slave-state legislatures to abandon slavery on their own. In November 1861, he devised a plan for the Northern slave state of Delaware that would offer government bonds as a buy-out if the Delaware legislature would put Delaware's slaves on a timetable for emancipation. (This was one reason why the Southern states seceded in 1861 — they rightly feared that Lincoln would manipulate them one-by-one into emancipation by similar schemes.)

Legislative emancipation, however, failed. Beginning with Delaware, the representatives of the four slave states remaining in the Union all rejected Lincoln's buy-out plan in 1862. That left Lincoln with only one other tool for emancipating the slaves, and that was his war-power as commander in chief. Before 1862, Lincoln was reluctant to use the war-power, partly because it was not very well understood as a legal concept; it might be upset by federal court decisions if enraged slaveholders tried to appeal "war-power" emancipation after the war. Such a proclamation could only apply legally to slaves in the areas actually in a state of war with federal authority.

Lincoln had already cancelled two attempted martial-law emancipations by John C. Fremont and David Hunter. But by the summer of 1862, Lincoln had no other way forward. On July 22, he presented a draft of a war-powers emancipation to his Cabinet, and was persuaded to hold it back until it could be released on the heels of a Union military victory. With the defeat of the Confederates at Antietam, Md., on September 17, Lincoln prepared a fresh version of the proclamation and released it on September 22nd. It took formal effect on January 1, 1863. Since it was a war-powers proclamation, Lincoln was forced to exclude from emancipation the slaves of the border states and the slaves living in areas of the South which had been reclaimed by the federal armies. As a legal document, it lacks the eloquence of Lincoln's other great state papers. Nevertheless, Lincoln considered it an "act of justice," and pronounced the slaves it liberated "henceforth and forever free."

Timeline	1861	_September 11_	Orders General John C. Fremont to modify his emancipation decree
	1862	_April 16_	Signs act abolishing slavery in the District of Columbia with compensation to loyal owners
		May 19	Nullifies General Hunter's martial law emancipation edict and urges the border states of Delaware, Kentucky, Maryland, and Missouri to accept gradual, compensated emancipation
		June 19	Signs law barring slavery from the federal territories
		July 12	Warns border-state members of Congress that slavery "will be extinguished by mere friction and abrasion — by the mere incidents of the war"
		July 22	Submits draft of Emancipation Proclamation to Cabinet
		August 14	Lincoln's Address on Colonization to a Deputation of Free Blacks
		September 22	Issues Preliminary Emancipation Proclamation
	1863	_January 1_	Issues Emancipation Proclamation

Lincoln's Initial Thoughts on Emancipation

President Lincoln's "paramount" duty, he wrote to *New York Tribune* editor Horace Greeley on August 22, 1862, was to restore the Union. "If I could save the Union without freeing any slave I would do it, and if I could save it by freeing all the slaves I would do it, and if I could save it by freeing some and leaving others alone I would also do that." Significantly, however, Lincoln wrote these words after writing a draft of an emancipation proclamation — a draft he was not yet ready to announce publicly. Nevertheless, even during the first year of the Civil War, President Lincoln hoped to put slavery on the course toward extinction.

In March 1862 Lincoln had considered ending slavery in the District of Columbia through a policy of gradual, compensated emancipation. This letter to Horace Greeley, marked "Private," was written six months before his final decision to issue the emancipation proclamation.

Executive Mansion,

Washington. March 24. 1862.

Hon. Horace Greeley—

My dear Sir:

Your very kind letter of the 16th, to Mr. Colfax, has been shown me by him. I am grateful for the generous sentiments and purposes expressed towards the administration. Of course I am anxious to see the policy proposed in the late special message, go forward; but you have advocated it from the first, so that I need to say little to you on the subject. If I were to suggest anything it would be that as the North are already for the measure, we should urge it persuasively, and not menacingly, upon the South. I am a little uneasy about the abolishment of slavery in this District, not but I would be glad to see it abolished, but as to the time and manner of doing it. If some one of the border-states would move fast, I should greatly prefer it; but if this can not be in a reasonable time, I would like the bill to have the three main features—gradual—compensation—and vote of the people— I do not talk to members of Congress on the subject, except when they ask me— I am not prepared to make any suggestion about confiscation— I may drop you a line hereafter.

Yours truly
A. Lincoln

Letter from Abraham Lincoln to Horace Greeley, March 24, 1862. (Courtesy of the Morgan Library and Museum, MA 6027)

*Abraham Lincoln
to Horace Greeley*

March 24, 1862

Private

Executive Mansion,
Washington, March 24, 1862

Hon. Horace Greeley.

My dear Sir:

Your very kind letter of the 16th to Mr. Colfax, has been shown me by him. I am grateful for the generous sentiments and purposes expressed towards the administration. Of course I am anxious to see the policy proposed in the late special message, go forward; but you have advocated it from the first, so that I need to say little to you on the subject. If I were to suggest anything it would be that as the North are already for the measure, we should urge it persuasively, and not menacingly, upon the South. I am a little uneasy about the abolishment of slavery in the District, not but I would be glad to see it abolished, but as to the time and manner of doing it. If some one or more of the border-states would move first, I should greatly prefer it; but if this can not be in a reasonable time, I would like the bill to have the three main features—gradual—compensation—and vote of the people. I do not talk to members of Congress on the subject, except when they ask me. I am not prepared to make any suggestion about confiscations. I may drop you a line hereafter.

Yours truly

A. Lincoln

John Jones was a Union soldier in Co. F, 45th Illinois Infantry. In this letter he responds enthusiastically to news reports that President Lincoln would issue an emancipation proclamation: "'The year of Jubilee' has indeed come to the poor Slave. . . . The name of Abraham Lincoln will be handed down to posterity as one of the greatest benefactors of his country."

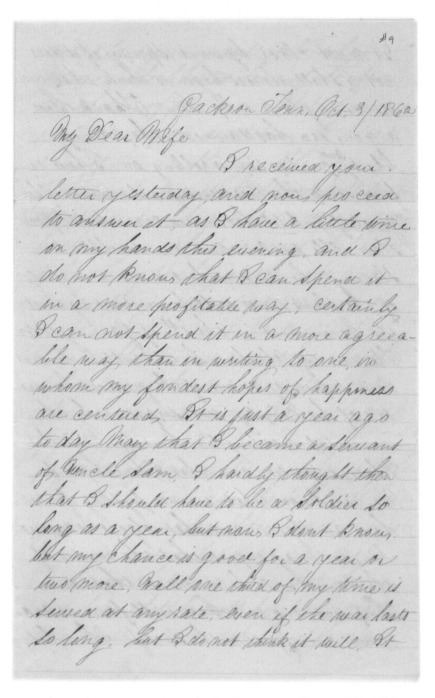

Letter from John P. Jones to his wife, October 3, 1862. Page 1. (The Gilder Lehrman Collection, GLC 5981.09)

*Excerpt from a
Letter from
John Jones to
his Wife*

October 3, 1862

Jackson Tenn. Oct. 3 / 1862

My Dear Wife

I received your letter yesterday, and now proceed to answer it, as I have a little time on my hands this evening, and I do not know that I can spend it in a more profitable way. certainly I can not spend it in a more agreeable way, than in writing to one, in whom my fondest hopes of happiness are centered. It is just a year ago to-day Mary that I became a Servant of Uncle Sam. I hardly thought then that I should have to be a Soldier so long as a year, but now I dont know but my chance is good for a year or two more. Well one third of my time is served at any rate, even if the war lasts so long, but I do not think it will. It <u>must</u> close by next spring, if it does not I shall almost begin to think that we never ought to whip them. Thank God a new era has dawned, the car of liberty [inserted: and] civilisation is rolling on. I have reference to the Presidents proclamation. The "<u>Year</u> <u>of</u> <u>Jubilee</u>" has indeed come to the poor slave. The proclamation is a deathblow to slavery, because without doubt a majority of the slave[s] states will be in arms against the Government on the 1st of January 1862.* The name of Abraham Lincoln will be handed down to posterity, as one of the greatest benefactors of his country, not surpassed by the immortal Washington himself. It is what I have expected, and what I have hoped for. We now know what we are fighting for, we have an object, and that object is avowed. Now we may expect that the armies of the Union will be victorious, that an Omnipotent and just God will favor us, and crown our efforts with success. Oh! what a day for rejoicing will it be, when America the boasted "land of the free and home of the brave" shall have erased from its fair escutcheon the black stain of human slavery. The majority of the people, and the soldiers will sustain the President in his act, it is well received by the army in this department, believed to be the right thing at the right time. . . .

* Jones wrote 1862 in error; the Emancipation Proclamation was issued on January 1, 1863.

The Emancipation Proclamation

The Emancipation Proclamation was shaped by both pragmatic considerations and Lincoln's deeply held, lifelong hatred of slavery. It was timed to strike a military blow against the South's economic and social infrastructure, and was taken in the full understanding (given the experience of "contrabands") that the advance of the Union armies would free more and more fugitive slaves.

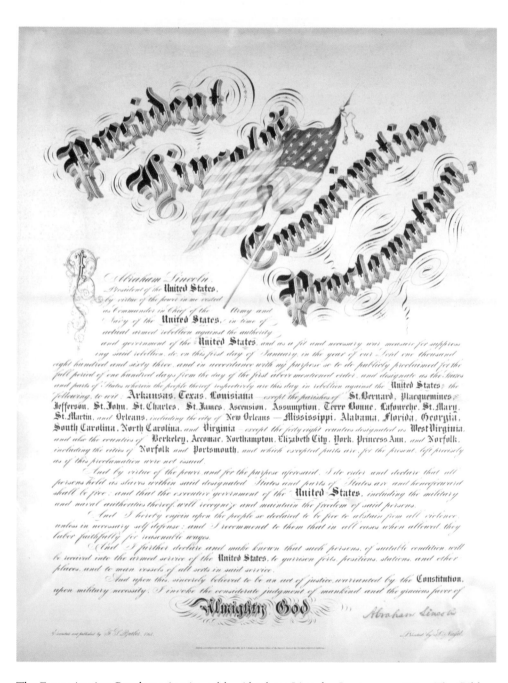

The Emancipation Proclamation issued by Abraham Lincoln, January 1, 1863. (The Gilder Lehrman Collection, GLC 742)

Abraham Lincoln,
"The Emancipation
Proclamation"

January 1, 1863

I, Abraham Lincoln, President of the United States, by virtue of the power in me vested as Commander in Chief, of the Army and Navy of the United States in time of actual armed rebellion against the authority and government of the United States, and as a fit and necessary war measure for suppressing said rebellion . . . do order and declare that all persons held as slaves within said designated States, and parts of States, are, and henceforward shall be free; and that the Executive government of the United States, including the military and naval authorities thereof, will recognize and maintain the freedom of said persons.

And I hereby enjoin upon the people so declared to be free to abstain from all violence, unless in necessary self-defence; and I recommend to them that, in all cases when allowed, they labor faithfully for reasonable wages.

And I further declare and make known, that such persons of suitable condition, will be received into the armed service of the United States to garrison forts, positions, stations, and other places, and to man vessels of all sorts in said service.

And upon this act, sincerely believed to be an act of justice, warranted by the Constitution, upon military necessity, I invoke the considerate judgment of mankind, and the gracious favor of Almighty God.

Opposing Views of Lincoln's Emancipation Proclamation in the Press

In an age before radio, television, and the Internet, many Americans received news and expressed their opinions about politicians and presidents through newspapers. Political cartoons appeared in newspapers and were sold individually as prints in shops, on street corners, and by mail. These cartoons are vivid, sharp, and offensive to our eyes. But they invite us to put aside twenty-first-century assumptions and look at events through the eyes of people living in the era.

"Writing the Emancipation Proclamation," a satiric etching by V. Blada [Adalbert J. Volck], c. 1864. (The Gilder Lehrman Collection, GLC 493.03)

Lincoln Drafting the Emancipation Proclamation

Political cartoon by Adalbert Volck, Baltimore, c. 1864

Adalbert Volck was a Confederate sympathizer living in Baltimore, Md. Volck depicts Lincoln writing the Proclamation with ink from a well held by the devil, while trampling the Constitution underfoot. On the walls are paintings of violent abolitionist John Brown and the bloody slave uprising in Santo Domingo.

"President Lincoln, Writing the Proclamation of Freedom"

Lithograph after a painting by David Gilmour Blythe Cincinnati, 1863

Lincoln sits in a flag-draped room at a table, with the Bible in his left hand and the Constitution in his lap. The room is filled with symbols that reaffirm the importance of his act: the scales of justice, the presidential oath, and petitions against slavery. Lincoln draws strength from Washington's sword.

"President Lincoln, writing the Proclamation of Freedom." Lithograph based on a painting by David Gilmour Blythe, printed by Ehrgott, Forbriger & Co., Cincinnati, Ohio. (Library of Congress Prints and Photographs Division)

SECTION VII

★

The Union Preserved: Toward Reconstruction

The Union Preserved: Toward Reconstruction

by Thavolia Glymph, Assistant Professor of African and African American Studies and History, Duke University

The Civil War ended in April of 1865 with two signal victories: the Union preserved and slavery on its way to complete extinction in the United States. Neither of these outcomes could have been predicted in 1861 when the war began or, for that matter, for two years into the war. Despite the North's vast advantage in population, material resources, industry, finance, railroads, communication, and naval power, a Union victory in the Civil War was not inevitable. Even after the momentous Union victories at Gettysburg, Penn., and Vicksburg, Miss., in July 1863, the war dragged on for more than a year and a half.

But by 1863, the tides were clearly shifting in favor of Union military victory and emancipation. Lincoln began to plan for the restoration of the Union. On January 1, 1863, he issued the Emancipation Proclamation, which, despite its practical limitations, transformed the war into a crusade to preserve the Union and to end slavery. Six months later, he rejected a proposal that would have allowed Louisiana to rejoin the Union without repudiating slavery.

In the end, victory was made possible by the active engagement of African Americans, both enslaved and free. The flight of African Americans from plantations, their eagerness to enlist in the U.S. Army, their willingness to endure atrocities exacted by Confederate soldiers, and their unfailing belief that the Union would endure helped to preserve the Union and shape its reconstruction.

A shift in military commanders and strategy played a pivotal role in the Union's eventual victory. In March 1864, President Lincoln gave Ulysses S. Grant command of all Union armies. Initially, Lincoln and his generals anticipated a conventional war in which Union soldiers would respect civilians' property. But as the war dragged on, the president and such officers as Grant and William Tecumseh Sherman believed that it was necessary to wage total war. Sherman said, "We are not only fighting hostile armies but a hostile people, and must make old and young, rich and poor, feel the hard hand of war."

Lincoln won reelection in 1864 after a campaign against General George McClellan. So concerned was he that he might be defeated, Lincoln gave furloughs to Union soldiers so that they might go home to cast their votes. The soldiers' votes were a key factor in several congressional races and in the adoption of a new state constitution in Maryland abolishing slavery. Actual victories on the battlefield, such as the capture of Atlanta in September 1864, were most decisive as far as the presidential race was concerned.

Lincoln's victory encouraged him to articulate his plan for reconstruction. In his Annual Message to Congress in December of 1864, he pointed to the establishment of loyal governments in Maryland, Arkansas, Louisiana, and other states as a step toward reconstruction. He lobbied actively for the passage of the Thirteenth Amendment abolishing slavery, which Congress passed in January 1865. In his Second Inaugural Address, Lincoln attributed the war to the "offense of slavery" and envisioned a Union of free citizens in which those who had seceded could return to a nation "with malice toward none, with charity for all."

Timeline	**1864**	*March 10*	Ulysses S. Grant appointed general-in-chief of the Union army
		June 8	Renominated as Republican Party's candidate for president
		September 2	General William Tecumseh Sherman's army captures Atlanta
		November 8	Reelected president with 212 of 233 electoral votes and 55 percent of the popular vote
		December 20	General Sherman reaches Savannah, Georgia, completing his march to the sea
	1865	*April 2*	Siege of Richmond by Union Army; Confederates evacuate
		April 9	Gen. Robert E. Lee surrenders to Gen. Ulysses S. Grant at Appomattox Court House in Virginia
		April 11	Makes his last public speech, which focuses on the problems of reconstruction
		April 14	Shot by John Wilkes Booth at Ford's Theatre in Washington, D.C., during the third act of *Our American Cousin*
		April 15	Dies at 7:22 a.m.
		May 4	Buried at Oak Ridge Cemetery outside Springfield, Illinois
		December 6	The Thirteenth Amendment to the U.S. Constitution, passed by Congress on January 31, 1865, is finally ratified. Slavery is abolished.
		December 13	Joint Committee on Reconstruction established by Congress

*Lincoln Develops a
Plan for Rebuilding
the Union*

Even before the Civil War ended, President Lincoln had begun to plan for the restoration of the Union. By mid-1863, Union forces exercised authority over most of Louisiana. In June 1863, a group of Louisiana planters asked the president to readmit the state to the Union with "all the rights . . . as they existed previous to . . . secession." Had President Lincoln agreed to this request, slavery would have survived in the state.

As the following letter to E. E. Malhiot, a Louisiana sugar planter, makes clear, Lincoln was not in a conciliatory mood. He would not allow Louisiana to reestablish its government unless it agreed to abolish slavery.

In December 1863, Lincoln offered a full pardon and restoration of rights to anyone who took an oath of loyalty, including a pledge to obey all Congressional laws pertaining to slavery. The president also declared that when the number of citizens taking the oath reached 10 percent of the votes cast in 1860, a rebellious state could form a new state government. Only those loyal to the Union would be allowed to vote and the new state constitution had to abolish slavery. In September 1864, Louisiana voters ratified a new constitution abolishing slavery.

*Excerpt from
a Letter from
Abraham Lincoln
to E. E. Malhiot
and others*

June 19, 1863

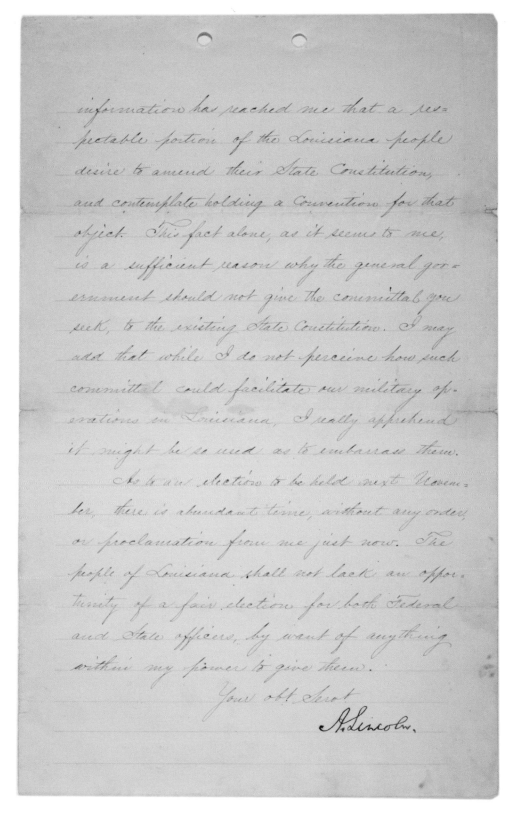

A letter to E. E. Malhiot and others signed by Abraham Lincoln, June 19, 1863. Page 3.
(The Gilder Lehrman Collection, GLC 1571)

*Excerpt from
a Letter from
Abraham Lincoln
to E. E. Malhiot
and others*

June 19, 1863

. . . Since receiving the letter, reliable information has reached me that a respectable portion of the Louisiana people desire to amend their State Constitution, and contemplate holding a Convention for that object. This fact alone, as it seems to me, is a sufficient reason why the general government should not give the committal you seek, to the existing State Constitution. I may add that while I do not perceive how such committal could facilitate our military operations in Louisiana, I really apprehend it might be so used as to embarrass them. As to an election to be held next November, there is abundant time, without any order, or proclamation from me just now. The people of Louisiana shall not lack an opportunity of a fair election for both Federal and State officers, by want of anything within my power to give them.

The Union
Victory Predicted

After the siege of Vicksburg, Mississippi on July 4, 1863, Lincoln came to see that Ulysses S. Grant had the strategic vision to win the war. In 1864, Lincoln brought Grant east to direct the war in Virginia. The resulting campaign involved six weeks of continuous fighting from May until mid-June. Grant then telegraphed Lincoln that he intended to cross the James River and attack Petersburg, the city protecting the Confederate capital of Richmond.

In this succinct and prophetic telegram Lincoln expresses his faith in General Grant's ability to ensure Union victory and end the war. He wrote this note in the early hours of the morning after a typical long night vetting incoming military reports.

A telegram from Abraham Lincoln to Ulysses S. Grant, June 15, 1864. (The Gilder Lehrman Collection, GLC1572)

Abraham Lincoln
to Ulysses S. Grant

June 15, 1864

Time Received _____

United States Military Telegraph,
War Department.

Washington, June 15, 1864

Lieut. Gen. Grant
Head Qrs. A. P.

Have just read your despatch of 1 p.m. yesterday. I begin to see it. You will succeed. God bless you all.

A. Lincoln

The 1864 Presidential Election

In the political turmoil of the times, Lincoln's Emancipation Proclamation was a courageous political statement that transformed the nation's war goals into a fight to end slavery. The Proclamation also reflected efforts to bring about the end of slavery by prominent African Americans and by acts of Congress. But the Proclamation weakened the Republican Party: in the Congressional elections of 1862, the party lost seats in Congress.

It was not inevitable that Lincoln would be elected to a second term as president in 1864. No president had been elected to a second term for thirty-two years. As late as the summer of 1864, Lincoln himself was convinced that he would be defeated. In a particularly demoralizing incident in July, Confederate General Jubal Early staged a surprise raid that struck within five miles of the White House.

Although President Lincoln won an overwhelming majority of the electoral votes in 1864 — receiving 212 to just 21 for his Democratic opponent, George B. McClellan — the popular vote was quite close. Despite the fact that eleven Confederate states did not participate in the election, Lincoln received just fifty-five percent of the popular vote in 1864. In three of the states that he carried (Connecticut, New York, and Pennsylvania), his margin of victory was only about three percent or less of the popular vote. Nevertheless, the election guaranteed that the Emancipation Proclamation would not be rescinded by a Democratic president.

The following document illustrates Lincoln's strategy of furloughing troops to return home to vote. This brought Lincoln's party stunning success in the state elections in October. General William Tecumseh Sherman's capture of Atlanta during the first week of September helped to swing the vote in Lincoln's favor.

Abraham Lincoln to Edwin M. Stanton

October 22, 1864

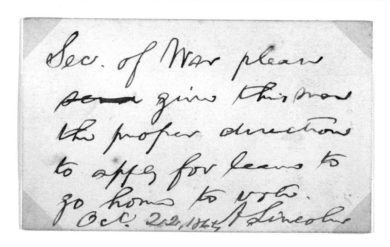

A note from Abraham Lincoln to Secretary of War Edwin M. Stanton, October 22, 1864. (The Gilder Lehrman Collection, GLC 4618)

Lincoln's Annual Message to Congress, 1864

Lincoln's annual messages to Congress — precursors of modern State of the Union Addresses — were comprehensive speeches on the affairs of the nation. In his fourth and final Annual Message, in December 1864, Lincoln touched on military operations before turning to recent Reconstruction efforts and plans for a reunified nation.

Lincoln's plan for reunification was based on the legal premise that the South had never really seceded, but that the government had only been suspended by treasonous individuals. On December 8, 1863, Lincoln issued a Proclamation of Amnesty and Reconstruction, which offered a full pardon and restoration of rights to anyone in rebellion against the Union who took an oath of loyalty. Included in the oath was a pledge to adhere to all laws passed by Congress in regard to slavery.

As the Union triumph approached, Lincoln looked towards the daunting goal of healing the war-torn nation. Outlining a lenient plan of Reconstruction, Lincoln focused on restoring and mending the nation rather than punishing the South.

These two speech fragments contain an important discussion of the status of Reconstruction efforts in the conquered territories and loyal border states. Lincoln also notes developments in three of the border slave states. As the abolition of slavery became linked to Union victory, these states served as a testing ground for levels of Southern resistance.

Note for Abraham Lincoln's annual message to Congress, December 6, 1864. (The Gilder Lehrman Collection, GLC3252)

Important movements have also occurred during the year to the effect of moulding society for durability in the Union. Although short of complete success, it is much in the right direction, that twelve thousand citizens in each of the States of Arkansas and Louisiana, have organized loyal State governments, with free constitutions, and are earnestly struggling to maintain and administer them. The movements in the same direction, more extensive, though less definite, in Missouri, Kentucky, and Tennessee, should not be overlooked.

Maryland, a bitterly divided state, had been occupied by Union troops since the beginning of the war, which hastened the disintegration of slavery and the mobilization of black resistance. Maryland Unionists had even implemented loyalty oaths for voters prior to Lincoln's amnesty proclamation. As a result Unionists committed to uncompensated and immediate emancipation dominated the state government in 1863. They called for a constitutional convention, where delegates constructed a new plan of government that abolished slavery. The constitution narrowly passed, but blacks remained disenfranchised and excluded from attending public schools.

Note by Abraham Lincoln for his annual message to Congress, December 6, 1864. (The Gilder Lehrman Collection, GLC5808)

[But Maryland] presents the example of complete success. Maryland is secure to liberty and Union for all the future. The genius of rebellion will no more claim Maryland. Like another unclean spirit, being driven out, it may seek to tear her, but it will woo her no more.

The Passage of the Thirteenth Amendment

In April 1864, the Senate, responding in part to an active abolitionist petition campaign, passed the Thirteenth Amendment to abolish slavery in the United States. Opposition from Democrats in the House of Representatives prevented the amendment from receiving the required two-thirds majority. The Emancipation Proclamation had freed only those slaves in states still at war. As a wartime order, it could subsequently be reversed by presidential decree, congressional legislation, or a court ruling. The permanent emancipation of all slaves therefore required a constitutional amendment.

Following his reelection, Lincoln threw his weight behind the amendment. In the end he persuaded eight House Democrats to switch their votes and encouraged several other Representatives who had missed the previous vote to support the amendment, which was finally passed on January 31, 1865, and was ratified by the states on December 6, 1865. It is the only constitutional amendment that was signed by a president. The Constitution does not require a president's signature; an amendment only needs to be approved by two-thirds of both Houses of Congress. With his signature, Lincoln placed the authority of his office behind the abolition of slavery throughout the United States.

Note by Abraham Lincoln for his annual message to Congress, December 6, 1864.
(The Gilder Lehrman Collection, GLC8094)

…At the last session of Congress a proposed amendment of the Constitution [*inserted above:* abolishing slavery throughout the United States,] passed the Senate, but failed for lack of the requisite two thirds vote in the House of Representatives. Although the present is the same congress, and nearly the same members, and without questioning the wisdom or patriotism of those who stood in opposition, I venture to recommend the reconsideration and passage of the measures at the present session.

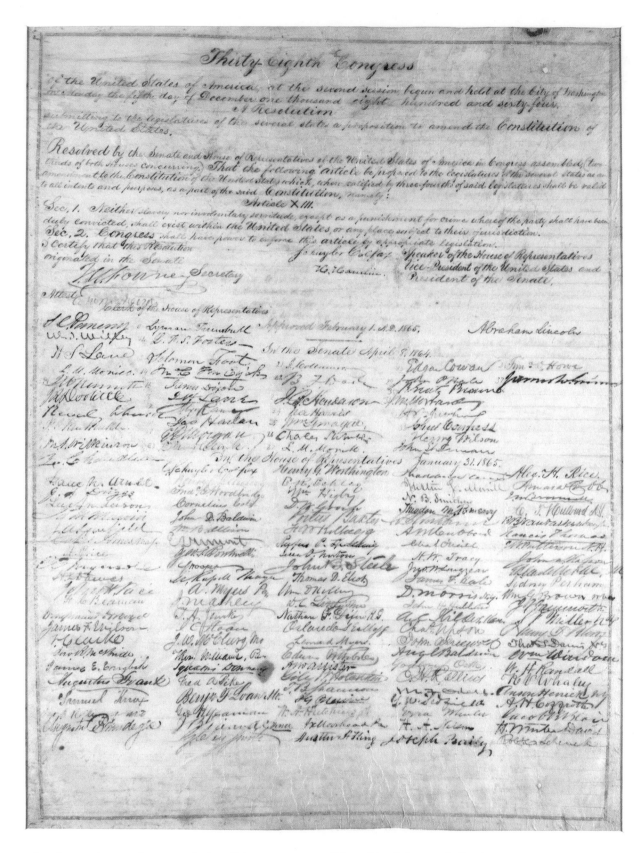

The Thirteenth amendment resolution, February 1, 1865. (The Gilder Lehrman Collection, GLC263)

Thirty-Eighth Congress

Of the United States of America, at the second session, begun and held at the City of Washington on Monday the fifth day of December one thousand eight hundred and sixty-four

A Resolution

Submitting to the legislatures of the several states a proposition to amend the Constitution of the United States.

Resolved by the Senate and House of Representatives of the United States of America in Congress assembled (two-thirds of both Houses concurring,) That the following article be proposed to the legislatures of the several states as an amendment to the Constitution of the United States which, when ratified by three-fourths of said legislatures shall be valid to all intents and purposes, as a part of the said Constitution, namely:

Article XIII.

Sec. 1. Neither slavery nor involuntary servitude, except as a punishment for crime whereof the party shall have been duly convicted, shall exist within the United States, or any place subject to their jurisdiction.

Sec.2. Congress shall have power to enforce this article by appropriate legislation.

I certify that this Resolution originated in the Senate	Schuyler Colfax	Speaker of the House of Representatives
J.W. Forney, Secretary	H. Hamlin.	Vice-President of the
Attest E McPherson		United States and
Clerk of the House of Representatives		President of the Senate,

Approved February 1. A.D. 1865. Abraham Lincoln

In the Senate April 8. 1864
[signatures of Senators]

In the House of Representatives January 31. 1865
[signatures of Representatives]

The Second Inaugural Address

Just 701 words long, Lincoln's Second Inaugural Address took only six or seven minutes to deliver, yet contains many of the most memorable phrases in American political oratory. The speech contained neither gloating nor rejoicing. Rather, it offered Lincoln's most profound reflections on the causes and meaning of the war. The "scourge of war," he explained, was best understood as divine punishment for the sin of slavery, a sin in which all Americans, North as well as South, were complicit. It describes a national moral debt that had been created by the "bondsmen's 250 years of unrequited toil," and ends with a call for compassion and reconciliation.

With its biblical allusions, alliteration, repetition, and parallel structure, and its reliance on one-syllable words, the address has the power of a sermon. It incorporates many of the themes of the religious revivals: sin, sacrifice, and redemption. At a White House reception, President Lincoln encountered Frederick Douglass. "I saw you in the crowd today, listening to my inaugural address," the president remarked. "How did you like it?" "Mr. Lincoln," Douglass answered, "that was a sacred effort."

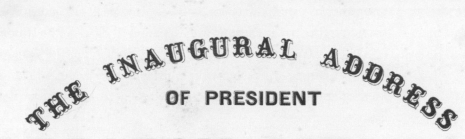

THE INAUGURAL ADDRESS

OF PRESIDENT

ABRAHAM LINCOLN,

DELIVERED AT THE NATIONAL CAPITOL,

MARCH 4th, 1865.

Fellow Countrymen:

At this second appearing to take the oath of the Presidential Office, there is less occasion for an extended address than there was at the first. Then a statement somewhat in detail of a course to be pursued seemed very fitting and proper. Now, at the expiration of four years, during which public declarations have been constantly called forth on every point and phase of the great contest which still absorbs the attention and engrosses the energies of the nation, little that is new could be presented.

The progress of our arms—upon which all else chiefly depends—is as well known to the public as to myself; and it is, I trust, reasonably satisfactory and encouraging to all. With high hope for the future, no prediction in regard to it is ventured.

On the occasion corresponding to this four years ago, all thoughts were anxiously directed to an impending civil war. All dreaded it; all sought to avoid it. While the inaugural address was being delivered from this place, devoted altogether to saving the Union without war, insurgent agents were in the city seeking to destroy it without war—seeking to dissolve the Union and divide the effects by negotiation.

Both parties deprecated war; but one of them would make war rather than let the nation survive, and the other would accept war rather than let it perish, and the war came.

One-eighth of the whole population were colored slaves, not distributed generally over the Union, but localized in the Southern part of it. These slaves constituted a peculiar and powerful interest. All knew that this interest was somehow the cause of the war. To strengthen, perpetuate and extend this interest was the object for which the insurgents would rend the Union by war, while the Government claimed no right to do more than to restrict the territorial enlargement of it.

Neither party expected for the war the magnitude or the duration which it has already attained. Neither anticipated that the cause of the conflict might cease, even before the conflict itself should cease. Each looked for an easier triumph and a result less fundamental and astounding.

Both read the same Bible, and pray to the same God, and each invokes His aid against the other. It may seem strange that any men should dare to ask a just God's assistance in wringing their bread from the sweat of other men's faces; but let us judge not, that we be not judged. The prayers of both should not be answered. That of neither has been answered fully. The Almighty has His own purposes. Woe unto the world because of offences, for it must needs be that offences come; but woe to that man by whom the offence cometh. If we shall suppose that American Slavery is one of these offences—which, in the providence of God, must needs come, but which, having continued through His appointed time, He now wills to remove, and that He gives to both North and South this terrible war as the woe due to those by whom the offence came—shall we discern there is any departure from those Divine attributes which the believers in a living God always ascribe to Him? Fondly do we hope, fervently do we pray, that this mighty scourge of war may speedily pass away. Yet, if God wills that it continue until all the wealth piled by the bondman's two hundred and fifty years of unrequited toil shall be sunk, and until every drop of blood drawn with the lash shall be paid by another drawn with the sword, as was said three thousand years ago, so still it must be said that the judgments of the Lord are true and righteous altogether.

With malice toward none, with charity for all, with firmness in the right, as God gives us to see the right, let us strive on to finish the work we are in, to bind up the nation's wound, to care for him who shall have borne the battle, and for his widow and orphans; to do all which may achieve and cherish a just and a lasting peace among ourselves and with all nations.

President Lincoln's Second Inaugural Address, March 4, 1865. (The Gilder Lehrman Collection, GLC6044)

...On the occasion corresponding to this four years ago, all thoughts were anxiously directed to an impending civil war. All dreaded it; all sought to avoid it. While the inaugural address was being delivered from this place, devoted altogether to saving the Union without war, insurgent agents were in the city seeking to destroy it without war—seeking to dissolve the Union and divide the effects by negotiation.

Both parties deprecated war; but one of them would make war rather than let the nation survive, and the other would accept war rather than let it perish, and the war came.

One-eighth of the whole population were colored slaves, not distributed generally over the Union, but localized in the Southern part of it. These slaves constituted a peculiar and powerful interest. All knew that this interest was somehow the cause of the war. To strengthen, perpetuate and extend this interest was the object for which the insurgents would rend the Union by war, while the Government claimed no right to do more than to restrict the territorial enlargement of it.

Neither party expected for the war the magnitude or the duration which it has already attained. Neither anticipated that the cause of the conflict might cease, even before the conflict itself should cease. Each looked for an easier triumph and a result less fundamental and astounding.

Both read the same Bible and pray to the same God, and each invokes His aid against the other. It may seem strange that any men should dare to ask a just God's assistance in wringing their bread from the sweat of other men's faces; but let us judge not, that we be not judged. The prayers of both should not be answered. That of neither has been answered fully. The Almighty has His own purposes. Woe unto the world because of offences, for it must needs be that offences come; but woe to that man by whom the offence cometh. If we shall suppose that American Slavery is one of these offences—which, in the providence of God, must needs come, but which, having continued through His appointed time, He now wills to remove, and that He gives to both North and South this terrible war as the woe due to those by whom the offence came— shall we discern there is any departure from those Divine attributes which the believers in a living God always ascribe to Him? Fondly do we hope, fervently do we pray, that this mighty scourge of war may speedily pass away. Yet, if God wills that it continue until all the wealth piled by the bondsman's two hundred and fifty years of unrequited toil shall be sunk, and until every drop of blood drawn with the lash shall be paid by another drawn with the sword, as was said three thousand years ago, so still it must be said that the judgments of the Lord are true and righteous altogether.

With malice toward none, with charity for all, with firmness in the right, as God gives us to see the right, let us strive on to finish the work we are in, to bind up the nation's wound, to care for him who shall have borne the battle, and for his widow and orphans; to do all which may achieve and cherish a just and a lasting peace among ourselves and with all nations.

The War Concludes

On April 4, 1865, two days after the Confederate capital of Richmond fell to Union forces, President Lincoln traveled there with his son Tad, who was celebrating his twelfth birthday that day. Lincoln entered the city without any fanfare. African Americans, however, greeted the President warmly.

The war ended on April 9, 1865, when Confederate General Robert E. Lee surrendered to Ulysses S. Grant at Appomattox Court House, in Virginia.

"The Room in McLean House at Appomattox C.H., in which Gen. Lee surrendered to Gen. Grant." A detail from a print by the Major & Knapp Engraving, Manufacturing & Lithographic Co., New York, NY, c.1867. (The Gilder Lehrman Collection, GLC 2979.01)

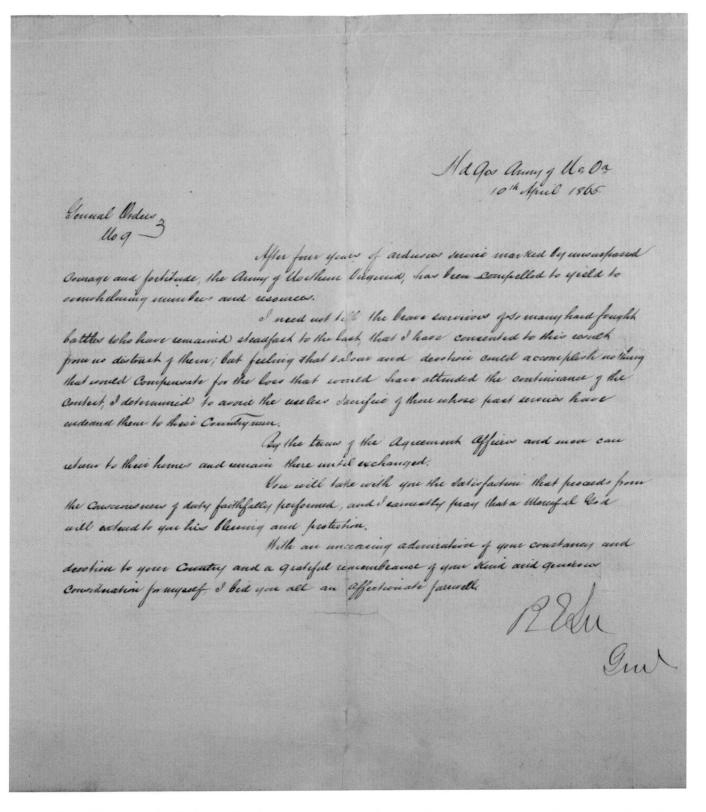

General Order No. 9, signed by Robert E. Lee, informing his men of the surrender at Appomattox, April 10, 1865. (The Gilder Lehrman Collection, GLC 1432)

Hd. Qrs. Army No.Va.

10th April 1865

General Order

No. 9

After four years of arduous service marked by unsurpassed courage and fortitude the Army of Northern Virginia, has been compelled to yield to overwhelming numbers and resources.

I need not tell the brave survivors of so many hard fought battles who have remained steadfast to the last, that I have consented to this result from no distrust of them; but feeling that valour and devotion could accomplish nothing that would Compensate for the loss that would have attended the continuance of the contest, I determined to avoid the useless sacrifice of those whose finest services have endeared them to their Countrymen.

By the terms of the agreement Officers and men can return to their homes and remain there until exchanged.

You will take with you the satisfaction that proceeds from the consciousness of duty faithfully performed, and I earnestly pray that a merciful God will extend to you his blessing and protection.

With an unceasing admiration of your constancy and devotion to your country and a grateful remembrance of your kind and generous consideration for myself, I bid you all an affectionate farewell.

R. E. Lee

Genl.

Abraham Lincoln's Last Speech

April 11, 1865

For many Americans, the most immediate impact of the war was the loss of the nation's greatest president. Lincoln's courageous leadership during the war had preserved a nation and ended slavery. On April 11, 1865, the president spoke publicly about his vision for rebuilding the nation with the help of four million formerly enslaved people. In the audience that day was John Wilkes Booth, a virulent racist who vowed to stop the man who promised citizenship for African Americans. Three days later, Booth murdered Lincoln and the trajectory of American history changed.

We meet this evening, not in sorrow, but in gladness of heart. The evacuation of Petersburg and Richmond, and the surrender of the principal insurgent army, give hope of a righteous and speedy peace whose joyous expression can not be restrained. In the midst of this, however, He from whom all blessings flow, must not be forgotten. A call for a national thanksgiving is being prepared, and will be duly promulgated. Nor must those whose harder part gives us the cause of rejoicing, be overlooked. . . .

By these recent successes the re-inauguration of the national authority — reconstruction — . . . is pressed much more closely upon our attention. It is fraught with great difficulty. Unlike a case of a war between independent nations, there is no authorized organ for us to treat with. . . . Nor is it a small additional embarrassment that we, the loyal people, differ among ourselves as to the mode, manner, and means of reconstruction. . . .

In the Annual Message of Dec. 1863 and accompanying Proclamation, I presented a plan of re-construction (as the phrase goes) which, I promised, if adopted by any State, should be acceptable to, and sustained by, the Executive government of the nation. . . . The new constitution of Louisiana, declaring emancipation for the whole State, practically applies the Proclamation to the part previously excepted. It does not adopt apprenticeship for freed-people; and it is silent, as it could not well be otherwise, about the admission of members to Congress. . . .

The amount of constituency, so to speak, on which the new Louisiana government rests, would be more satisfactory to all, if it contained fifty, thirty, or even twenty thousand, instead of only about twelve thousand, as it does. It is also unsatisfactory to some that the elective franchise is not given to the colored man. I would myself prefer that it were now conferred on the very intelligent, and on those who serve our cause as soldiers. . . .

Some twelve thousand voters in the heretofore slave-state of Louisiana have sworn allegiance to the Union, assumed to be the rightful political power of the State, held elections, organized a State government, adopted a free-state constitution, giving the benefit of public schools equally to black and white, and empowering the Legislature to confer the elective franchise upon the colored man. Their Legislature has already voted to ratify the constitutional amendment recently passed by Congress, abolishing slavery throughout the nation. These twelve thousand persons are thus fully committed to the Union, and to perpetual freedom in the state. . . .

The Assassination

On Good Friday, April 14, 1865, Lincoln attended a performance of the play *Our American Cousin* at Ford's Theatre in Washington, D.C. Shortly after 10 p.m., John Wilkes Booth entered the presidential box and shot Lincoln in the head before leaping to the stage and shouting "sic semper tyrannis" ("thus always to tyrants"). Lincoln died nine hours later, on Saturday, April 15, at 7:22 in the morning.

Immediately following the assassination, martial law was imposed and Washington's roads and bridges were closed. An immense $100,000 reward was offered for the conspirators' capture. Hundreds of suspects were taken into custody. For twelve days, Booth and an accomplice successfully eluded Union forces. Finally, on April 26, 1865, Booth was cornered in a barn in Virginia. When he refused to surrender, pursuing troops set fire to the structure. Sergeant Boston Corbett shot Booth fatally in the neck.

News of Lincoln's death sent shockwaves and expressions of grief across the nation. This poster reproduces a telegram sent by Secretary of War Edwin Stanton to Major General John Dix, military commander of the Department of the East in New York City. The large font of the poster reflects its use as a public announcement posted on the streets of New York.

"The President is Dead!"

April 15, 1865

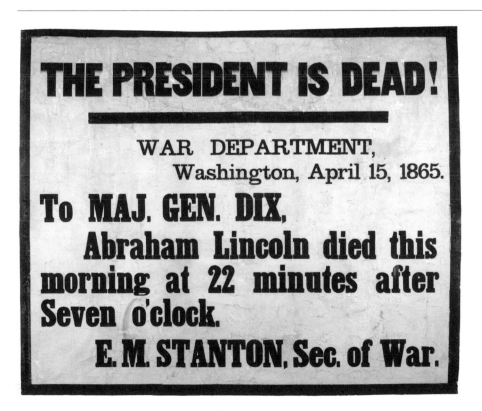

Broadside announcing Lincoln's death, April 15, 1865. (The Gilder Lehrman Collection, GLC 6680)

SECTION VIII

Abraham Lincoln's Enduring Legacy

Abraham Lincoln's Living Legacy

*by David W. Blight,
Class of 1954
Professor of American
History, Yale University*

Lincoln's controversial, crucial, and enduring significance in American history will always be linked to the question of emancipation. This is a case where events, ideas, and human character combined to produce a world-changing historical outcome. Writing in 1922, stressing the sixteenth president's capacity to grow, the great African American scholar W.E.B. Du Bois wrote one of the most telling statements of Lincoln's legacy on emancipation. "I love him," wrote Du Bois, "not because he was perfect, but because he was not and yet triumphed. . . . The world is full of folk whose taste was educated in the gutter. The world is full of folk born hating and despising their fellows. To these I love to say: See this man. He was one of you and yet became Abraham Lincoln."

Du Bois saw to the core of Lincoln as a leader of both frustrating paradox and deep humanity. "There was something left," Du Bois wrote of Lincoln, "so that at the crisis he was big enough to be inconsistent — cruel, merciful, peace-loving, a fighter, despising Negroes and letting them fight and vote, protecting slavery, and freeing slaves. He was a man — a big, inconsistent, brave man." Lincoln's brave inconsistency, along with the bravery of Union forces made up of black and white soldiers, as well as the sheer courage of slaves themselves, made the Civil War what Frederick Douglass ultimately termed an "abolition war." Without Lincoln at the center, that outcome could have been very different.

Timeline

1865	*March 3*	Congress establishes the Freedman's Bureau.
	April 14	On Good Friday, John Wilkes Booth shoots President Abraham Lincoln at Washington's Ford's Theater. As he leaps to the stage (breaking a shinbone), Booth shouts, "Sic Semper Tyrannis (Thus Always to Tyrants)." Lincoln died the next morning. Andrew Johnson becomes the 17th president
	December 6	The Thirteenth Amendment to the U.S. Constitution abolishes slavery
1866	*April 9*	Congress passes the Civil Rights Act over President Andrew Johnson's veto, granting citizenship and civil rights to all persons born in the United States (except Native Americans) and providing for the punishment of those who violate those rights
1867	*March 2*	The first Reconstruction Act imposes martial law on the southern states, splits them into five military districts, and provides for the restoration of civil government when they ratify the 14th Amendment
1868	*February 24*	The House of Representatives votes to impeach President Andrew Johnson. The Senate trial lasted 11-and-a-half weeks. On the major charges, the Senate voted 35-19 for conviction, one vote short of the 2/3 vote required for removal from office
	July 28	The 14th Amendment to the U.S. Constitution grants citizenship to anyone born in the United States and guarantees due process and equal protection of the laws
1870	*February 25*	Hiram R. Revels of Mississippi becomes the first African American to serve in the U.S. Senate. Joseph H. Rainey of South Carolina becomes the first black Representative

	March 30	The 15th Amendment to the U.S. Constitution guarantees the right to vote regardless "of race, color, or previous condition of servitude"
1875	*March 1*	Congress passes the Civil Rights Act of 1875 to guarantee equal use of public accommodations and places of public amusement. It also forbids the exclusion of African Americans from jury duty. In 1883, the Supreme Court declares the act unconstitutional, ruling that states, but not private individuals, are forbidden from discriminating on the basis of race.
1877	*February 27*	An electoral commission declares Rutherford Hayes the winner of the disputed presidential election. On April 10, President Hayes begins to withdraw federal troops from the South, marking the official end to Reconstruction.
1881		Tennessee segregates railroad cars. Thirteen southern states adopt similar segregation statutes by 1907.
1890	*November 1*	Mississippi restricts black suffrage by requiring voters to demonstrate an ability to read and interpret the U.S. Constitution. Seven other southern states institute similar plans by 1910.
1896	*May 18*	Plessy v. Ferguson. The U.S. Supreme Court rules that segregation of blacks and whites was permitted under the Constitution so long as both races receive equal facilities.

The combined effects of Lincoln's Emancipation Proclamation and the collapse of the political and economic power of the South opened a new world for both blacks and whites.

However, Reconstruction would test the limits of idealism, and, as early as 1863, civilians were reporting the challenges facing freed slaves in the South. In this letter, the Western Sanitary Commission informs President Lincoln that many freed slaves in the Mississippi Valley were lacking in provisions, clothing, bedding, and cooking supplies. To meet the emergency, Commission members experienced in caring for the sick and wounded offered to volunteer "to prevent or lessen the sufferings of the coming winter and spring." The WSC accumulated $30,000 in clothing and other necessary materials as well as $13,000 in cash to assist the communities along the Mississippi. In recognition of the WSC's contributions, Lincoln later asked James Yeatman, the Commission's president, to run the Freedman's Bureau.

LETTER TO THE PRESIDENT OF THE UNITED STATES.

ROOMS WESTERN SANITARY COMMISSION,
St. Louis, November 6th, 1863.

His Excellency, A. LINCOLN,
President of the United States.

SIR:— The undersigned, members of the Western Sanitary Commission, most respectfully represent, that the condition of the Freed Negroes in the Mississippi Valley is daily becoming worse, and calls most loudly upon the humane and loyal people of the Northern States for help. There are probably not less than fifty thousand, chiefly women and children, now within our lines, between Cairo and New Orleans, for whom no adequate provision has been made. The majority of them have no shelter but what they call "brush tents," fit for nothing but to protect them from night dews. They are very poorly clad—many of them half naked—and almost destitute of beds and bedding—thousands of them sleeping on the bare ground. The Government supplies them with *rations*, but many unavoidable delays arise in the distribution, so that frequent instances of great destitution occur. The army rations (*beef and crackers*) are also a kind of diet they are not used to; they have no facilities of cooking, and are almost ignorant of the use of wheat flour; and even when provisions in abundance are supplied, they are so spoiled in cooking as to be neither eatable nor wholesome. Add to these difficulties, the helplessness and improvidence of those who have always been slaves, together with their forlorn and jaded condition when they reach our lines, and we can easily account for the fact that sickness and death prevail to a fearful extent. No language can describe the suffering, destitution and neglect which prevail in some of their "camps." The sick and dying are left uncared for, in many instances, and the dead unburied. It would seem, now, that one-half are doomed to die in the process of freeing the rest.

Our purpose is not to find fault, but to seek for the remedy. Undoubtedly, Congress must take the matter in hand, to mature plans of permanent relief; but, judging from past experience, a good many months will elapse before its final action, and there will still remain a great deal that properly belongs to private charity, and for which legislation cannot provide.

To meet the present exigency, and to prevent or lessen the sufferings of the coming winter and spring, we offer our humble but active services, asking no reward of any kind, but the opportunity and encouragement to work. Our experience for two and a-half years past, in the sanitary cause of the sick and wounded, has taught us the lessons of economy and prudence, and we are too much accustomed to difficulties to be discouraged by them. It may not be unbecoming in us to say, in recommending ourselves for the work proposed, that in the two years from October, 1861, to November, 1863, we have received and expended for the sick and wounded of the Western Army, in stores or money, to the amount of a million and a quarter of dollars, and that the total expenses of distribution, including all salaries and incidental charges, has been but little in excess of *one per cent*. For the manner in which the work has been done, and the good results accomplished, we refer to Major-Generals Grant, Sherman, Steele, Schofield, Curtis, Fremont, and to the Commander-in-Chief, Major-General Halleck. We also refer to Assistant Surgeon-General, Col. R. C. Wood, and to all members of the Medical Staff of the West, with whom and under whose direction we have always worked.

We now respectfully ask permission and authority to extend our labors to the suffering freed people of the South-West and South. If you will give us your endorsement in the undertaking before the people, we think we can raise large sums of money, and accomplish great good. Nor would it be only a work of philanthropy, but equally of patriotism, for it would remove an increasing reproach against the Union cause, and by lessening the difficulties of emancipation, would materially aid in crushing the rebellion. At present, hundreds of the blacks would gladly return to slavery, to avoid the hardships of freedom; and if this feeling increases and extends itself among them, all the difficulties of the situation will be increased; while, at the same time, a most effective argument is given to the disloyal against our cause.

We most respectfully leave the subject before you, feeling sure that you will agree with us as to the necessity of prompt and energetic action, And have the honor to remain,
Your cordial friends and obedient servants,
JAMES E. YEATMAN,
GEORGE PARTRIDGE,
JOHN B. JOHNSON,
CARLOS S. GREELEY,
WILLIAM G. ELIOT.

Broadside of a letter to President Abraham Lincoln from the Western Sanitary Commission, November 6, 1863.
(The Gilder Lehrman Collection, GLC1545.11)

Rochester. N.Y. August 17. 1865.

Mrs Abraham Lincoln:

Dear Madam: Allow me to thank
you, as I certainly do thank you most sincerely for
your thoughtful kindness in making me the owner
of a Cane— which was formerly the property and the
favorite walking staff of your late lamented husband. the
honored and venerated President of the United States.

I assure you, that this inestimable memento of his
Excellency will be retained in my possession while I live
— an object of sacred interest— a token not merely of
the kind consideration in which I have reason to know
that, President was pleased to hold me personally, but
as an indication of his humane ~~consideration~~ interest
welfare of my whole race.

With every proper sentiment of Respect and Esteem
I am, Dear Madam, your Obd.t Serv.t

Frederick Douglass.

A letter from Frederick Douglass to Mary Lincoln, August 17, 1865. (The Gilder Lehrman Collection, GLC 2474)

In the early years of the war and just preceding it, Frederick Douglass had criticized Lincoln for failing to move or speak decisively for emancipation. However, over the course of the war, and despite initial differences, Douglass and Lincoln forged a relationship based on a shared vision. After Lincoln's assassination, Douglass wrote Mrs. Lincoln to thank her for the gift of the President's favorite walking stick.

Frederick Douglass to Mary Todd Lincoln

August 17, 1865

Rochester, N.Y. August 17. 1865.

Mrs Abraham Lincoln:

Dear Madam: Allow me to thank you, as I certainly do thank you most sincerely for your thoughtful kindness in making me the owner of a cane which was formerly the property and the favorite walking staff of your late lamented husband, the honored and venerated President of the United States.

I assure you, that this inestimable meumento of his Excellency will be retained in my possession while I live — an object of sacred interest — a token not merely of the kind consideration in which I have reason to know that the President was pleased to hold me personally, but ~~of~~ as an Indication of [*inserted:* his] ~~the~~ humane interest [in the] welfare of my whole race.

With every proper sentiment of Respect and Esteem
I am, Dear Madam, your Obed^t Ser^vt
Frederick Douglass.

Constitutional Recognition of Emancipation's Promise of Freedom

The passage of the Thirteenth, Fourteenth and Fifteenth Amendments gave constitutional status to emancipation's promise of freedom. Here legislation takes symbolic form. The artist depicts African Americans' hopes arising from the passage of the Fifteenth Amendment in 1870: education, family life, jobs, and the vote. Among the collage of images are portraits of Frederick Douglass, John Brown, and Abraham Lincoln.

"The Fifteenth Amendment, Celebrated May 19, 1870." (The Gilder Lehrman Collection, GLC 2917)

A Monument for Abraham Lincoln

Eleven years after Lincoln's death, Douglass gave his most considered comments on the late president's racial attitudes. Speaking at the unveiling of a statue of Lincoln and a kneeling former slave in Washington, D.C., paid for largely by former slaves, he offered a highly nuanced view of Lincoln's relationship with blacks. For Douglass, Lincoln's cautious approach to emancipation represented the only way that four million slaves might have been liberated.

Statue of Emancipation Monument by sculptor Thomas Ball, in Lincoln Park, Washington, D.C., photographed by J. F. Jarvis, November 13, 1876. (Library of Congress Prints and Photographs Division)

Excerpt from an
Oration by Frederick
Douglass Delivered
on the Occasion
of the Unveiling
of the Freedmen's
Monument
in Memory of
Abraham Lincoln

Lincoln Park,
Washington, D.C.
April 14, 1876

Friends and fellow-citizens, the story of our presence here is soon and easily told. We are here in the District of Columbia, here in the city of Washington, the most luminous point of American territory; a city recently transformed and made beautiful in its body and in its spirit; we are here in the place where the ablest and best men of the country are sent to devise the policy, enact the laws, and shape the destiny of the Republic; we are here, with the stately pillars and majestic dome of the Capitol of the nation looking down upon us; we are here, with the broad earth freshly adorned with the foliage and flowers of spring for our church, and all races, colors, and conditions of men for our congregation—in a word, we are here to express, as best we may, by appropriate forms and ceremonies, our grateful sense of the vast, high, and pre-eminent services rendered to ourselves, to our race, to our country, and to the whole world by Abraham Lincoln. . . .

When, therefore, it shall be asked what we have to do with the memory of Abraham Lincoln, or what Abraham Lincoln had to do with us, the answer is ready, full, and complete. Though he loved Caesar less than Rome, though the Union was more to him than our freedom or our future, under his wise and beneficent rule we saw ourselves gradually lifted from the depths of slavery to the heights of liberty and manhood; under his wise and beneficent rule, and by measures approved and vigorously pressed by him, we saw that the handwriting of ages, in the form of prejudice and proscription, was rapidly fading away from the face of our whole country; under his rule, and in due time, about as soon after all as the country could tolerate the strange spectacle, we saw our brave sons and brothers laying off the rags of bondage, and being clothed all over in the blue uniforms of the soldiers of the United States; under his rule we saw two hundred thousand of our dark and dusky people responding to the call of Abraham Lincoln, and with muskets on their shoulders, and eagles on their buttons, timing their high footsteps to liberty and union under the national flag; under his rule we saw the independence of the black republic of Hayti, the special object of slaveholding aversion and horror, fully recognized, and her minister, a colored gentleman, duly received here in the city of Washington; under his rule we saw the internal slave-trade, which so long disgraced the nation, abolished, and slavery abolished in the District of Columbia; under his rule we saw for the first time the law enforced against the foreign slave-trade, and the first slavetrader hanged like any other pirate or murderer; under his rule, assisted by the greatest captain of our age, and his inspiration, we saw the Confederate States, based upon the idea that our race must be slaves, and slaves forever, battered to pieces and scattered to the four winds; under his rule, and in the fullness of time, we saw Abraham Lincoln, after giving the slaveholders three months' grace in which to save their hateful slave system, penning the immortal paper, which, though special in its language, was general in its principles and effect, making slavery forever impossible in the United States. Though we waited long, we saw all this and more. . . .

Fellow-citizens, I end, as I began, with congratulations. We have done a good work for our race today. In doing honor to the memory of our friend and liberator, we have been doing highest honors to ourselves and those who come after us; we have been fastening ourselves to a name and fame imperishable and immortal; we have also been defending ourselves from a blighting scandal. When now it shall be said that the colored man is soulless, that he has no appreciation of benefits or benefactors; when the foul reproach of ingratitude is hurled at us, and it is attempted to scourge us beyond the range of human brotherhood, we may calmly point to the monument we have this day erected to the memory of Abraham Lincoln.

Photograph of Frederick Douglass, c. 1870. (The Gilder Lehrman Collection, GLC 5111.01.1318)

A Birthday Tribute to Abraham Lincoln

Booker T. Washington's earliest memory was of his mother praying that Abraham Lincoln would succeed in ending slavery. But Lincoln did not end slavery on his own. Pressure for emancipation came from a handful of field commanders, Republicans in Congress, abolitionists, free blacks, and slaves themselves, who played a pivotal role in their own liberation. During the war, many enslaved African Americans contributed to their own emancipation by deserting plantations and fleeing to Union lines. Wartime resistance to slavery also took the form of work stoppages, arson, sabotage, and isolated cases of murder. Enlistment in the Union army represented the most dramatic form of resistance. In August 1862, the first slave regiment was formed, the 1st South Carolina Volunteers, and by the war's end, 186,000 blacks — three quarters of them former slaves — served in the Union army, and another 20,000 in the navy, accounting for nearly ten percent of all Union forces and 68,178 of the Union dead or missing. Nevertheless, Lincoln's role in slavery's abolition was crucial. His Emancipation Proclamation transformed the Civil War from a war for union into a war of liberation, and his wholehearted support helped insure ratification of the Thirteenth Amendment, abolishing slavery.

Excerpt from a Speech by Booker T. Washington, on the Centennial of Lincoln's birth

New York Republican Club February 12, 1909

I was born a slave.

My first recollection of Abraham Lincoln was on this wise. I was awakened early one morning before the dawn of day as I lay wrapped in a bundle of rags on the dirt floor of our slave cabin by the prayers of my mother, just before leaving for the day's work, as she was kneeling over my body earnestly praying that Abraham Lincoln might succeed and that one day she and her boy might be free. You give me an opportunity here this evening to celebrate with you and the Nation the answer to that prayer.

Lincoln Address -1-

Feb-12-1909

Republican Club of New York City

which
You ask that he found a piece of property and turned into a free American citizen

to speak to you to-night of Abraham Lincoln. I am not fitted by history or training

to be your teacher to-night for, as I have stated, I was born a slave.

My first recollection of Abraham Lincoln was on this wise. I was awakened early

one morning before the dawn of day as I lay wrapped in a bundle of rags on the dirt

floor of our slave cabin by the prayers of my mother, just before leaving for the day's

as she
work, was kneeling over my body earnestly praying that Abraham Lincoln might succeed

and that one day she and her boy might be free. You give me an opportunity here this

evening to celebrate with you and the Nation the answer to that prayer.

Says the Great Book,
Though a man die, yet shall he live. If this is true of the ordinary man, how much

more true is it of the hero of the hour and the hero of the century—Abraham Lincoln.

One hundred years of the life and influence of Lincoln is but the repetition of the story

of the struggles, the trials, ambitions and triumphs of those composing our complex

American civilization. Interwoven into the warp and woof of it all is the graphic story

nearly
of men and women of every race and color, representing their progress from slavery to

freedom, from poverty to wealth, from weakness to power, from ignorance to intelligence.

Knit into the life of Abraham Lincoln is the story and success of the Nation in the

blending of all tongues, religions, colors, races, into one composite Nation, leaving

each group and race free to live its own separate social life and yet all a part of the

great whole.

Typed manuscript of a speech draft by Booker T. Washington, February 12, 1909. Page 1. (The Gilder Lehrman Collection, GLC 7232)

To Learn More

Questions
for Discussion

SECTION I / *Lincoln: The Formative Years*

1. Based upon his early life, would you have expected Abraham Lincoln to rise to a position of prominence and eventually be elected president? Explain.

2. How do the documents in this section illustrate Lincoln's values and character? Give specific examples.

3. How do the letters to Johnston and Latham demonstrate Lincoln's belief in self-improvement and the American dream?

SECTION II / *The Emergence of Lincoln the Politician*

1. Choose a document that illustrates the influence of Lincoln's principles on his actions as a politician.

2. How did Lincoln respond to key events of the 1850s? Review the documents in this section to identify events that influenced the formation of the Republican Party.

3. Did Lincoln have a clear and consistent policy toward slavery? Support your answer with specific examples from the documents.

SECTION III / *Lincoln and the Election of 1860*

1. Read the Cooper Institute Address. How did Lincoln express his support for the Constitution and his opposition to slavery?

2. a) Create a political map showing states won and lost by Lincoln.
   b) How does this map help illustrate the impact of sectionalism in 1860?

3. Analyzing the data in *Lloyd's New Political Chart*, explain why Lincoln was called "the minority president."

4. Would you characterize Lincoln's Springfield speech as optimistic? Explain.

SECTION IV / *Lincoln's Presidency*

1. Read the First Inaugural Address. Was war inevitable?
    Support your view with specific examples.

2. How did Lincoln deal with the crisis of secession?

3. Read the documents about Lincoln as commander of the armed forces.
    How involved was he in the daily management of the war?

4. Why is the Gettysburg Address considered one of the best and most
    important speeches in American history?

SECTION V / *Lincoln and Race*

1. Based on a reading of the documents in this section, do you think Lincoln's
    views on race and slavery evolved over time?

2. Read the document "Abraham Lincoln on Nathaniel Gordon's Request
    for Clemency," and explain why Lincoln refused to commute the slave
    trader's death sentence.

3. Twentieth-century civil rights leaders looked to Lincoln for inspiration.
    What specific documents in this section might have influenced them?

SECTION VI / *Lincoln and Emancipation*

1. Explain how the two images in this section reflect opposing views
    of Lincoln's Emancipation Proclamation.

2. Who was the intended audience for the Emancipation Proclamation?
    Examine the document and explain.

3. Why was the Emancipation Proclamation written in a much more legalistic
    fashion than the Gettysburg Address?

4. Does Lincoln's correspondence prior to the Emancipation Proclamation give
    us a clue to his feelings regarding slavery? Explain.

SECTION VII / *The Union Preserved: Toward Reconstruction*

1. How do the documents in this section provide insight into Lincoln's views about the conduct of war, reconstruction, and the re-integration of the South into the Union?

2. Supporters of the Confederacy claimed that if the Union triumphed, Lincoln and his Republican supporters would seek revenge upon the South. Based on the documents in this section, were the Confederate supporters correct? Explain and support your answer.

3. Using the documents in this section, trace the increased concern shown by Lincoln for the condition and treatment of African Americans.

SECTION VIII / *Abraham Lincoln's Enduring Legacy*

1. Using the lithographic image *The Fifteenth Amendment Celebrated*, identify five basic rights gained by African Americans as a result of the Fifteenth Amendment to the Constitution.

2. Based on the comments by James Yeatman, why could the Freedmen's Monument be called "the people's monument"?

3. Many former slaves referred to President Lincoln as "Father Abraham." To what extent does the Frederick Douglass oration support or refute this view?

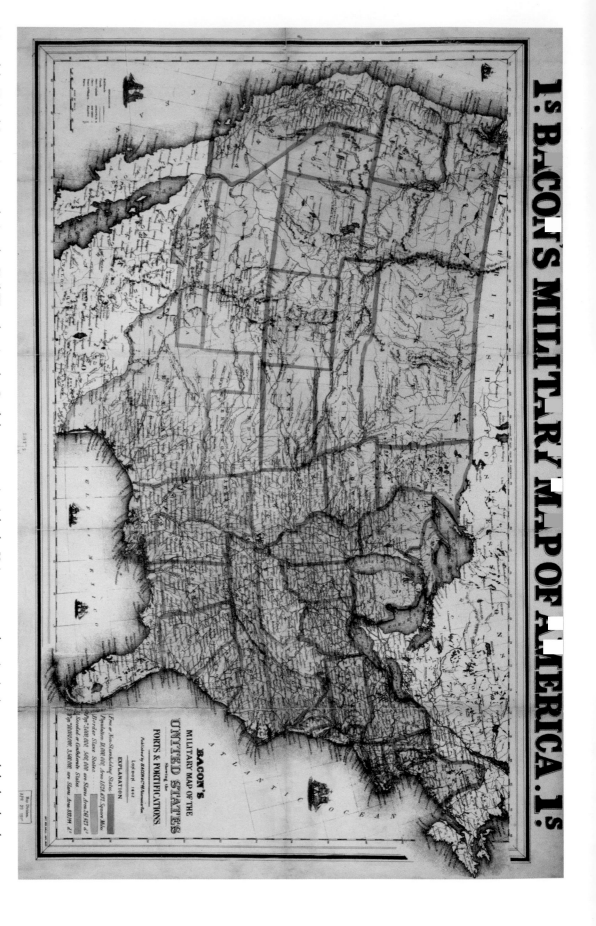

Map of the United States in 1862, during the Civil War, showing the Confederate states in pink, the Union states and territories in green, and the border slave-holding states and territories in yellow (London, 1862). (Courtesy of the Library of Congress Geography and Map Division)

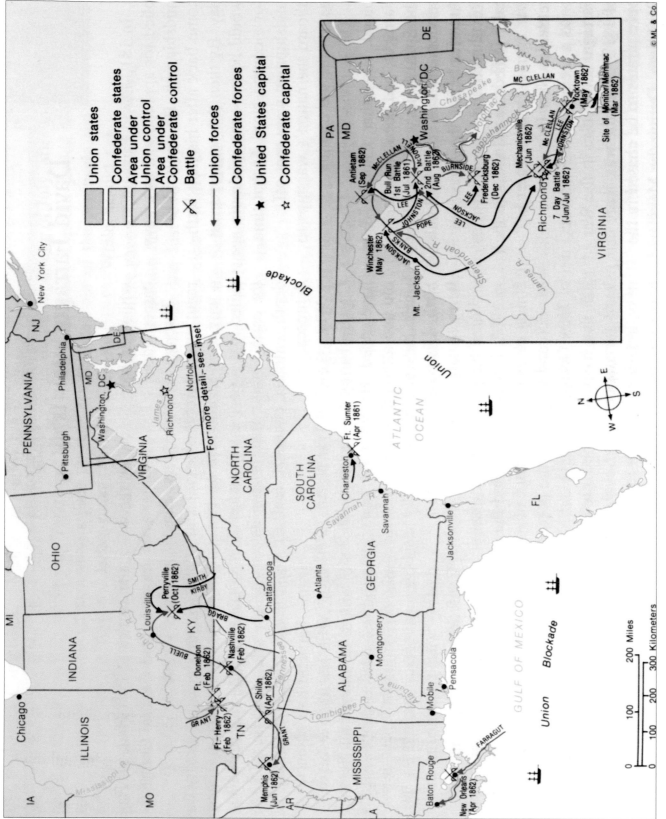

Major campaigns and battles during the Civil War, 1861–1862. (Used by permission of McDougal Littell Inc., a division of Houghton Mifflin)

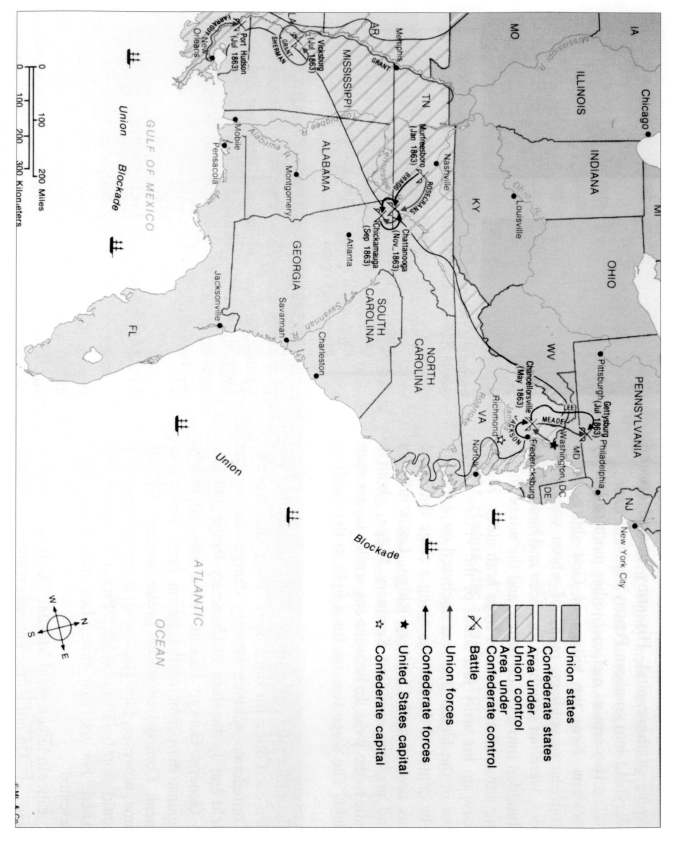

Major campaigns and battles during the Civil War, 1863. (Used by permission of McDougal Littell Inc., a division of Houghton Mifflin)

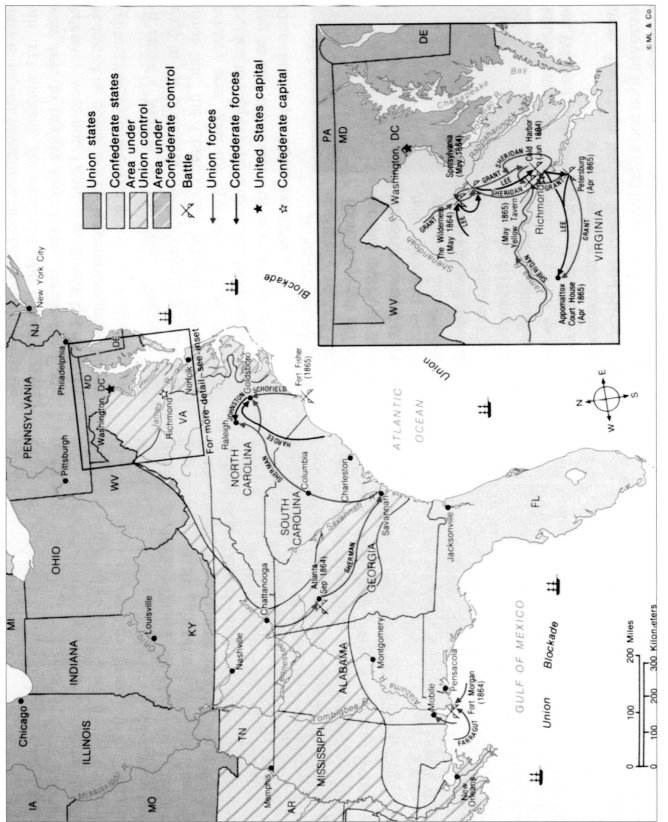

Major campaigns and battles during the Civil War, 1864-1865. (Used by permission of McDougal Littell Inc., a division of Houghton Mifflin)

Teaching Strategies

The most effective way to learn history is to do history. Doing history requires each of us to become a historical detective or investigator. All students, regardless of grade level, have the ability to be historians — to identify important historical questions and to piece together the past out of its surviving fragments. Only in this way can a student develop a genuine mastery of the past.

The serious study of history involves three distinct skills:

1. **Identifying a Historical Problem:** History isn't simply an attempt to reconstruct the past; it is also an effort to answer questions and solve problems.

2. **Discovering and Evaluating Evidence:** Historical research begins with primary sources — the surviving remnants of the past. These can be texts — such as letters, diaries, newspaper articles, and legal records — or they can be physical, visual, or oral evidence — music, paintings, photographs, and many other kinds of artifacts. Evidence does not speak for itself; rather, it must be carefully analyzed and interpreted.

3. **Drawing and Presenting Conclusions:** The final step is to bring one's insights and evidence to bear on the historical problem and to present one's findings in a clear, succinct, and persuasive form.

*The Gilder Lehrman
Institute of
American History
Document Analysis
Worksheet*

1. Type of document (check one)

   ☐ Image   ☐ Report to Congress

   ☐ Private letter   ☐ Map

   ☐ Political cartoon   ☐ Newspaper

   ☐ Speech or public address   ☐ Telegram

   ☐ Other (describe) _____

   _____

2. Date(s) of document _____

   _____

3. Author(s) _____ _____

   _____

4. Document Information

   A. List important pieces of information in the document.

   B. Why was the document written?

C. What evidence in the document helps you to determine why it was written? (Use quotations if appropriate.)

D. What historical event(s) does this document refer or pertain to?

E. On a scale of 1-10 how would you rate the importance of this document? Explain why.

Recent Books

Gabor S. Boritt
The Gettysburg Gospel: The Lincoln Speech that Nobody Knows
> Gabor Boritt draws on little-known documents to recreate the details of November 19, 1863, when President Abraham Lincoln dedicated a new national cemetery. The Gettysburg Gospel is a fascinating assessment of the events preceding and following Lincoln's address. Boritt illustrates how this speech, which has become the most famous in American oratory, took on new meaning in subsequent decades.

Richard Carwardine
Lincoln: A Life of Purpose and Power
> In this, the most important biography of the 16th president since David Herbert Donald's 1995 *Lincoln*, an Oxford historian emphasizes Abraham Lincoln's political skills and his philosophical convictions — his unwavering commitment to Union, his repugnance toward slavery, and his belief that no one, regardless of race, should be denied the fruits of their own labor.

Doris Kearns Goodwin
Team of Rivals: The Political Genius of Abraham Lincoln
> This book explores how Lincoln succeeded in winning the Republican presidential nomination over candidates with larger national reputations and then created an effective wartime cabinet filled with men who had been his political rivals.

Allen C. Guelzo
Abraham Lincoln: Redeemer President
> An intellectual biography that analyzes the evolution of the 16th president's moral, political, and religious beliefs.

Allen C. Guelzo
Lincoln's Emancipation Proclamation: The End of Slavery in America
> An authoritative account of the origins of the Emancipation Proclamation and its impact on slaves, on American relations with Europe, and on the conduct of the Civil War. This book explains why it took Lincoln nearly two years to issue the Proclamation, why the document's language is so uninspired, and why Lincoln limited emancipation to specific parts of the South.

William Lee Miller

Lincoln's Virtues: An Ethical Biography

Not a biography in the conventional sense, this book traces the development of Lincoln's character, psychology, and morality. The central question it asks is how the son of illiterate pioneers achieved greatness. It examines how he developed the eloquence and skills of political leadership that characterized his presidency.

Merrill Peterson

Lincoln in American Memory

This volume traces the transformation in Lincoln's place in American literature, art, and memory, paying particular attention to the evolution of such notions as Lincoln as the "Great Emancipator," as "Savior of the Union," as "Self-Made Man," and as "Martyr to the Cause of Freedom."

Douglas L. Wilson

Honor's Voice: The Transformation of Abraham Lincoln

This book traces Lincoln's transformation, between 1831 and 1842, from a small-town store clerk into a prominent attorney and member of the Illinois General Assembly, poised for national prominence.

Websites

America's Reconstruction
http://www.digitalhistory.uh.edu/reconstruction/index.html
> With text by Eric Foner, and featuring images from the Chicago Historical Society, the Valentine Museum in Richmond, and other leading historical collections, this online exhibition presents an up-to-date portrait of a period marked by unrealized goals of economic and racial justice that still confront our society.

The Collected Works of Abraham Lincoln
http://www.hti.umich.edu/l/lincoln/
> An online version of Roy P. Basler's eight-volume edition of *The Collected Works of Abraham Lincoln*, which was published between 1953 and 1955.

History Now: Issue on Abraham Lincoln (December 2005)
http://www.historynow.org/12_2005/index.html
> This quarterly online journal published by the Gilder Lehrman Institute of American History contains articles by noted historians as well as lesson plans, resource guides, and links to related websites. This special issue contains the following essays:

> "The Emancipation Proclamation: Bill of Lading or Ticket to Freedom?"
> by Allen C. Guelzo

> "Lincoln and Whitman"
> by David S. Reynolds

> "Lincoln's Civil Religion"
> by George C. Rable

> "Lincoln at Cooper Union"
> by Harold Holzer

> "Lincoln and Abolitionism"
> by Douglas L. Wilson

A House Divided: America in the Age of Lincoln
http://www.digitalhistory.uh.edu/ahd/index.html
> Featuring text by Columbia University historian Eric Foner and Olivia Mahoney, Director of Historical Documentation from the Chicago Historical Society, this online exhibition explores the causes and consequences of the Civil War. It treats the Civil War both as a military conflict and as a catalyst for far-reaching changes in American life.

Lincoln/Net
http://lincoln.lib.niu.edu/
> This site, created by Northern Illinois University in cooperation with the University of Chicago, the Newberry Library, the Chicago Historical Society, Illinois State University, the Illinois State Archives, Lewis University, and Knox College, contains campaign music and video interviews with leading historians, as well as extensive primary source texts, over 1,500 images and maps, and other resources relating to Lincoln's Illinois years.

Mr. Lincoln's Virtual Library
http://lcweb2.loc.gov/ammem/alhtml/alhome.html
> This Library of Congress site includes *The Abraham Lincoln Papers*, which contains approximately 20,000 items including correspondence and papers accumulated primarily during Lincoln's presidency; and *"We'll Sing to Abe Our Song!"* which includes more than two hundred sheet-music compositions that represent Lincoln and the war as reflected in popular music.

The Valley of the Shadow
http://valley.vcdh.virginia.edu/
> This digital archives details life in two American communities, one Northern and one Southern, from the time of John Brown's raid through the era of Reconstruction. It contains thousands of original letters and diaries, newspaper articles, speeches, and census, church, and military records from Augusta County, Virginia, and Franklin County, Pennsylvania.

Civil War / Lincoln Historic Sites

Abraham Lincoln Birthplace
National Historic Site
Hodgenville, KY
www.nps.gov/abli

Andersonville National Historic Site
Andersonville, GA
www.nps.gov/ande

Andrew Johnson National Historic Site
Greeneville, TN
www.nps.gov/anjo

Antietam National Battlefield
Sharpsburg, MD
www.nps.gov/anti

Appomattox Court House
National Historical Park
Appomattox, VA
www.nps.gov/apco

Arkansas Post National Memorial
Gillett, AR
www.nps.gov/arpo

Arlington House,
The Robert E. Lee Memorial
Arlington, VA
www.nps.gov/arho

Battleground National Cemetery
(Rock Creek Park)
Washington, DC
www.nps.gov/batt

Boston African American
National Historic Site
Boston, MA
www.nps.gov/boaf

Brices Cross Roads
National Battlefield Site
Baldwyn, MS
www.nps.gov/brcr

Chickamauga & Chattanooga National
Military Park
Fort Oglethorpe, GA
www.nps.gov/chch

Clara Barton National Historic Site
Glen Echo, MD
www.nps.gov/clba

Cumberland Gap
National Historical Park
Middlesboro, KY
www.nps.gov/cuga

Ford's Theatre National Historic Site
Washington DC
www.nps.gov/foth

Fort Circle Parks (Rock Creek Park)
Washington, DC
www.nps.gov/archive/rocr/ftcircle

Fort Donelson National Battlefield
Dover, TN
www.nps.gov/fodo

Fort Foote
Prince Georges County, MD
www.nps.gov/fofo

Fort McHenry National Monument
and Historic Shrine
Baltimore, MD
www.nps.gov/fomc

Fort Pickens (Florida Unit,
Gulf Islands National Seashore)
Pensacola Beach, FL
www.nps.gov/guis

Fort Pulaski National Monument
Savannah, GA
www.nps.gov/fopu

Fort Scott National Historic Site
Fort Scott, KS
www.nps.gov/fosc

Fort Sumter National Monument
Charleston Harbor, SC
www.nps.gov/fomo

Fort Warren (Georges Island,
Boston Harbor Islands
National Recreation Area)
Boston, MA
www.nps.gov/boha

Fort Washington Park
Fort Washington, MD
www.nps.gov/fowa

Frederick Douglass National Historic Site
Washington, DC
www.nps.gov/frdo

Fredericksburg & Spotsylvania National
Military Park
Fredericksburg, VA
www.nps.gov/frsp

General Grant National Memorial
New York, NY
www.nps.gov/gegr

Gettysburg National Military Park
Gettysburg, PA
www.nps.gov/gett

Glorietta Pass
(Pecos National Historical Park)
Pecos, NM
www.nps.gov/peco

Harpers Ferry National Historical Park
Harpers Ferry, WV
www.nps.gov/hafe

Kennesaw Mountain
National Battlefield Park
Kennesaw, GA
www.nps.gov/kemo

Lincoln Boyhood National Memorial
Lincoln City, IN
www.nps.gov/libo

Lincoln Home National Historic Site
Springfield, IL
www.nps.gov/liho

Lincoln Memorial
Washington, DC
www.nps.gov/linc

Manassas National Battlefield Park
Manassas, VA
www.nps.gov/mana

Monocacy National Battlefield
Frederick, MD
www.nps.gov/mono

Natchez National Historical Park
Natchez, MS
www.nps.gov/natc

Pea Ridge National Military Park
Pea Ridge, AR
www.nps.gov/peri

Petersburg National Battlefield
Petersburg, VA
www.nps.gov/pete

Richmond National Battlefield Park
Richmond, VA
www.nps.gov/rich

Shiloh National Military Park
Shiloh, TN
www.nps.gov/shil

Springfield Armory
National Historic Site
Springfield, MA
www.nps.gov/spar

Stones River National Battlefield
Murfreesboro, TN
www.nps.gov/stri

Tupelo National Battlefield
Tupelo, MS
www.nps.gov/tupe

Ulysses S Grant National Historic Site
St. Louis, MO
www.nps.gov/ulsg

Vicksburg National Military Park
Vicksburg, MS
www.nps.gov/vick

Wilson's Creek National Battlefield
Republic, MO
www.nps.gov/wicr

The Gilder Lehrman Institute of American History

Founded in 1994, the Gilder Lehrman Institute of American History promotes the study and love of American history. The Institute serves teachers, students, scholars, and the general public. It helps create history-centered schools and academic research centers, organizes seminars and enrichment programs for educators, produces print and electronic publications and traveling exhibitions, sponsors lectures by eminent historians, and administers a History Teacher of the Year Award in every state through its partnership with Preserve America. The Institute also conducts awards including the Lincoln, Frederick Douglass, and George Washington Book Prizes, and offers fellowships for scholars to work in the Gilder Lehrman Collection and other archives.

The Institute maintains two websites, www.gilderlehrman.org and the quarterly online journal www.historynow.org.